Day-to-Day Living with Mental Illness

ISBN-13: 978-1974225958

ISBN-10: 197422595X

Registration Number: TXu 2-038-696

Printed in USA

Dedication

This book is dedicated to all the sufferers out there.

Table of Contents

Disclaimer to reader:

Everything in this piece is verbatim to the writer's diary. The subject wishes to remain anonymous.

Patient was eighteen years old when these entries were documented. Patient's treating diagnosis in 2002, according to the DSM IV, is Dysthymia (300.4), Social Phobia (300.23), OCD(300.3) in a Borderline Personality (301.83) with a Learning Disability (Not otherwise Specified) (315.9).

Re Dysthymia: Depressed mood, irregular sleep, episodic anhedonia, and difficulty concentrating.

Re Anxiety: Obsessional pre-occupations, and psychogenic headaches and pains.

Re BPD: Pre-occupied with death, suicidal threatening, risk-taking behavior, poor affect tolerance, impaired reality testing under stress.

Preface

During my high school years in 1996 I had a nervous breakdown. I was fearful of the principal and I had depersonalization. I had thought at the time that it was just dizziness but it was indeed the beginning of the end. In 1998, I started intense psychotherapy that was insight oriented. I became in touch with my emotions but I had developed suicidality as a way to cope with the increased intensity or the awareness of the intensity of my emotions. I started drumming in the year 1999—finally developing a passion in life that I've never had before. But all that came to an end once September 11th 2001 terrorist attack was brought upon America. I was deeply affected and felt I needed to get in as much practice as possible—you never know when the end of the world will be. I started to over-practice playing the drums and hurt my wrists. After that, I couldn't drum anymore. At this point I was intensely suicidal and I had no reason to go on living. I got into smoking pot at this point and that initially was counterproductive but then wound up being a way of self-medicating. I ran into a host of problems with the withdrawal of the marijuana.

Part One

Identity

March, 2000 (Age 18)

I am really ready to stab myself with that sharp metal piece. I don't care if I die right now. This is a sick life I have. Why do I have to be different? No one can accept that I am different.

Dr. M. and I talked about the time I listened to a Metallica song and I got a headache. Dr. M. said that it's because I'm angry at the people that were the cause of me being created and having me be required to do the impossible with keeping the religion.

I felt like blaming my mother by reminding her that she shouldn't have had such a big family. I felt like taking it out on my mother, but my mother has been working so hard in buying a new house, I didn't feel like blaming it on her.

Dr. M. said that I don't cause myself depression by programming my mind to be that way. I make it bigger by obsessing about it and make it a bigger deal than it is. The depression comes because I have a sickness and I obsess because I have that sickness. He said that sometimes I use the depression as an excuse to not do anything. The thing is, I think, when you're depressed you don't feel like doing anything. When I come to the point of killing myself, during a depressed state, it's because I let myself get into the depression. If I didn't get more into the depression, maybe I wouldn't come to want to kill myself.

There are five things that bring on the primary depression, said Dr. M. One: I get headaches when I get into learning or excited about something. Two: I can't get control over my sex life and I don't have a girl or feel I could have a relationship with a girl. He suggested that I am so scared that I won't be able to satisfy her and that she's pretty and better than me. Three: I can't think clearly about religion. Four: I obsess a lot because of my OCD and when I doubt things; it makes me feel frustrated and hopeless since it's taking control of me. Five: I start to doubt whether I am going through anything and if I am sick.

All these things cause me frustration and to have a feeling of helplessness. There is no hope. I start to feel depressed. When I dwell on the depression by thinking about it, it's secondary depression. That I bring on because of self-pity. The times that I take it out on my mother are secondary. (Presently, I don't think it's profound of Dr. M. to say this about secondary depression, that I let myself get into the depression by thinking about it.)

Is the reason I am so angry with my mother because she goes around like there's nothing wrong with me and that I picked up on that kind of behavior? I think all I want is for her to accept me and respect me. I try to earn her respect. She keeps on avoiding the negativity because it's too painful. She told me that she feels it's too painful to consider me sick. I keep feeling that she doesn't respect me. I guess because she's expecting me to be like everyone else. Like a normal person. I was on the train and I saw some people that I knew. They asked me what I was doing. I told them that I have a learning disability with processing information. They said I don't look like I have that problem when I talk to them. It seemed that way because I didn't have any problem processing what they were saying at the moment. They said everyone has trouble processing information. I saw that these people probably have a similar problem as I, and they are doing fine with their work, since they are in computer school. I started to obsess that I don't have these problems and I am slowing myself down with learning because I think I have a learning disability; therefore I require less of myself. Maybe I should require more of myself. (It's hard to determine what I have because it's not like a strep test where it comes out positive or negative.)

Dr. M. said I do get more nervous than the average person. I think about the GED test and I might not pass it. And I might forget the material. So I feel like I have to keep going over it or I'll forget it. It's one thing to go over it, but to constantly feel like I have to go over it isn't normal. My teacher tells me that I should go over the material so that I won't forget it, because the test is three weeks away. But I can't go over everything. Thinking that I have to go over everything makes me stressed out and I don't know what to do. There are times I feel calm, after feeling nervous, and I don't accept feeling calm because I don't feel like it's the real me so I get back into the stressful thought process of worrying. Sometimes I don't get caught up in worrying about things, but I think it's the medication.

April, 2000 (Age 18)

Today I felt like killing myself. I started picturing myself bleeding and my father found me. I was depressed because I am worrying so much about school and tests. I realize that the exercises that Dr. M. gave me only help when I have something else to focus on with my mind. In school, I could tell myself, "What does it matter that I fail the test?" Then I get involved in the work again. But when I'm bored, this cognitive exercise doesn't work.

I'm through with life. I get so frustrated that I go crazy. When I start obsessing, I can't take it. Life is too fucking hard. It really is confusing because Dr. M. said I have OCD and severe anxiety disorder. All my friends don't think it's a big deal, as my learning disability teacher said, "Take your stress and put it on a shelf and forget about it". It seems as though I'm easily persuaded—I start doubting my problem is real even though my doctor said it is.

September, 2000 (Age 18)

I went to Dr. M today. He clarified something about my OCD. Compared to all of his patients and friends, I have a really bad case of anxiety disorder. The doubting I have is because of the anger caused by having OCD. I protect myself by doubting whether I have this problem or not. Dr. M says that my mind works in a way in which I need to experience symptoms of OCD 100% of the time in order for me to qualify it as a disorder. However, it is possible to have OCD and also have relief at times and it still does not mean I don't have it at all. (This currently makes me think about people in today's society that think in all or nothing terms with regard to political beliefs. A person believing a political candidate has redeemable qualities but that somehow cancels out the imperfections of the individual. I think the human brain is wired to have all or nothing thinking even if the person does not have a mental illness.)

January, 2001 (Age 18)

I feel that psychotherapy has really screwed me over. My OCD is worse. My depression is much worse. I'm even worrying that my suicidal thinking was caused by psychotherapy. I think it was. I didn't have it before. Before, all I had was depression. I don't think I have been helped. If anything, I am more into the anxiety and depression. Psychotherapy has made me focus too much on my problems and they feel even harder to deal with, even impossible. I don't know what to do. Now I have a new worry. That's fucking great.

I read a book called, "Obsessive Compulsive Disorders". In the book it mentions certain people that behavioral therapy might not work for. That would be someone who has low tolerance for frustration and doesn't have patience for the hard working process of behavioral therapy, which usually takes up to six to eight months. I don't have the patience for that especially since I don't see any progress. After a week, the anxiety isn't lowered significantly enough to want to go further. If I felt I can get some quicker relief, then I would have the motivation to continue.

I can't stand when a man loves a woman. They want to make a family. Now they have kids. The kids have to take responsibility for their lives. The problem is that the kids didn't ask for the responsibility. It's not a fair deal. I am stuck because I don't feel it's fair that, just because my parents had me come into this world, I have to take responsibility. I don't want to because I didn't ask for it. And I am angry that I have it against my will. I refuse to take responsibility for my life, but I won't kill myself to avoid having my family suffer. So, I will start smoking and taking drugs to cut my life short. I will get my money from my savings and I will not go ahead and get myself a job or get all crazy about it. I am in a big mess. I don't want responsibility and I have no tolerance for stress and will never have because I hate stress. I just like to relax. Besides, I didn't make the problem of me being in this world. I would like to die now and nobody has the right to stop me. I am miserable. I think I will cut down my visits to Dr. M. to once a week since I don't want to work on myself at all.

I like the anger. It feels good. It's very pleasurable. I guess that is the nature of it. It just makes you feel good; and when you're happy, you'd rather be happy than sad. And when I'm upset, I'd rather remain upset than happy. While I'm feeling happy, I realize that it isn't that great, because then I have to worry about whether my pot smoking interferes with my medication. I start to get anxious whether it does. I'd rather not worry about it and continue to enjoy myself.

If I decided to live life instead of being self-destructive, it doesn't mean I have to be involved in society, for example, going through the stress of getting a job and being employed. I could choose living without stress. I could kill time by drumming, smoking and bicycle riding -all the things I enjoy doing besides for working, which I don't like. I wouldn't enjoy the benefits of working because I'd be too overwhelmed with the accompanied stress. In general, I feel reluctant to relax. It's like I feel comfortable being anxious, so that I could be excused from responsibility. But the reason I want to be excused in the first place, is because it really is overwhelming when I considered taking a job.

I feel it's possible that there is a god in the world, but he's out to get us to make our lives as miserable as possible. He must get a kick out of making our existence hell on Earth; not for everyone as some people have it good. But a lot of people suffer.

All of my emotions—anger and fear—seem to skyrocket. All of these emotions come to a point where my mind cannot handle it. It gets too intense. I get a headache or I wind up not feeling or being aware of these emotional responses. I get too involved. I guess it's the chemical imbalance in my brain that results in disorders like OCD. This causes problems for my brains ability to regulate the intensity of the emotions— overwhelming my mind. Whatever it is that stops emotions from going to extremes seem to not be functioning, exaggerating emotions to a degree that I just can't handle them. I don't look like I'm overreacting, but I sure do feel it.

Part Two

Damaged

2003

Why do I have to be at the mercy of my feelings which overwhelm me to the point of me not thinking clearly? Anxiety brings on this form of psychosis where there is mental confusion and alongside, it is also obsessional because my confused thoughts keep repeating in my head and I am feeling unaware that the thoughts or my chains of thoughts are repetitious and intrusive. So anxiety now brings on a new form of mental illness for me which seems to be a form of psychosis or mental confusion. The anxiety is more frustrating now than before I started smoking pot. Now my problems and my life are going to be a living hell to deal with. Imagine having mental confusion about yourself and it being repeated in your mind over and over because you feel like you need and want to analyze yourself.

It seems my mind works with basically the same thoughts that pop up. For example, 'Oh shit, the weed is fucking up my brain'. The highs were similar to ecstasy. Maybe it did cause me to have the abnormalities that ecstasy can have on the brain.

I feel embarrassed about repeatedly playing the same songs on the piano and the drums. Being able to memorize the beat very well and play very well is a real success for me. I can't take the way people react to my talent. They say, "Wow! You have such a talent", or, "You're amazing!" I don't want to hear about the complements people give me about their appreciation for me.

I was shoveling the snow on the roof. There was just too much snow; I couldn't deal with it. I have forgotten that I get overwhelmed easily. I haven't really been experiencing it because I haven't been involved much in the world work-wise. I am so confused about what the problem with getting overwhelmed is. The weed relaxes me mentally and rids me of overwhelming feelings towards life. When I smoke, I don't really care so much about things. The snow on the roof is temporarily less overwhelming, at least until I need to smoke again.

I can get too nervous to even deal with trying to fix my drum set. I feel suddenly depressed and it lasts all day. I'm feeling confused or unfocused and want to sleep all day. I wish life would come to an end. The ending of life seems like a refuge from this horrible pain that I feel from this hopeless feeling. You can't understand how my feelings can hurt so badly. It is hopeless in a sense; I am too nervous when I drum in front of people. I'm too nervous to even sound good, too nervous to put feeling into the music because of the complements I may get.

Instead of getting self-destructive under stress, now I get disconnected. I feel so confused that I don't know what my problem is and I get obsessional. These days I get into a state of confusion instead of getting just suicidal. My mind works differently now because of the pot smoking. My life took a turn to a different direction; maybe in a little better direction since I can drum. The stress of life gets me disconnected or to think unclearly instead of suicidal. I guess it's better to disconnect than to get suicidal. But disconnecting makes me want just that.

I am really fucked up. I am not thinking clearly. I am not focused. It used to be that I didn't feel focused when I stopped smoking weed for over a week. Now I feel unfocused most of the time. I will have to smoke the rest of my life, which hopefully won't be too long. The only relief I get is not getting stuck on checking things. I am so nervous that I couldn't drum for the past week because I'm so afraid I am disturbing my family with them hearing me drum.

The Zyprexa seems to help with my disorganized thinking. It helps me think more clearly. My life sucks. I was given a bad deal. Every time there is stress in my life, like the thought of having to have to be on Medicaid to pay for meds, I worry about it and start having disorganized thinking. If I have to be housebound I will go crazy. I can't stay home everyday smoking weed; I need to get out.

I am trying to taper off the weed slowly. First I am going to smoke every other day for a month and then less and less. I don't know if I can do that. When I decide not to smoke today but smoke the next day, I obsess about smoking to a point where I just want to smoke now.

I'm not going to bother tapering off the weed because it caused nightmares. In my dream I felt such hatred towards my mother. I am feeling restless most of the time. I can't sit and watch a movie. I don't have patience until I smoke; then I can sit in one place.

I know I can't stop smoking weed. It's hard to believe that when I withdrew from smoking, I became psychotic. I felt like a vegetable. I couldn't think. This symptom is still somewhat present even though I started smoking again. Smoking marijuana is definitely addicting, especially if done every day for a long time. I am addicted.

I feel weak because of the Zyprexa. I can't live with this weakness; it's too much. It's hard to walk to the park or play the drums. Only on some days do I have the energy to walk or drum.

I don't know what is going on with me. I don't know if Elena helped me or not. I feel unfocused. I just can't figure anything out. I think that the weed really fucked with my mind when I stopped smoking and stopped thinking straight. I became vulnerable to a mental illness called Psychosis. I was relieved of the symptoms when I contacted Elena. Now it seems that things are generally getting better, but I'm still suffering greatly. For one thing, I can't play the drums in peace. I am always worrying that it's disturbing my family. Ever since I've been taking the Zyprexa, my psychotic-like symptoms have lessened. Though, I don't feel like I am thinking clearly. At least I'm not going to be here long. I am hoping that I will die soon. I've had enough of this shitty life. I am ready to die!

Whether or not the weed caused damage doesn't really matter since I left a message on Elena's answering machine. I've been feeling a little better, not 100% better, but good enough. Until I called Elena, my situation was getting worse. The marijuana caused me to be nervous, now it's not and I wasn't able to play the drums. My obsessions are at bay since the call. Elena's healing was short-lived. I had to call her again. I am not feeling better. However, I was able to drum tonight. I wasn't able to drum this morning.

Previously, under stress I would get overwhelmed but I still had a head on my shoulders. I would get increasingly obsessional, feeling unsettled all the time like I needed to check things. That was a living hell. Now, I get confused when I am under stress. This takes a toll on my intelligence and also on my being able to read books—too many words and details. I have big-time problems focusing on details. It saddens me to think that all this happened because I stopped smoking marijuana. Right now, my illness is more complex than ever before. I guess it was a trade-off when I started smoking. I traded OCD with psychosis. I still have the OCD especially with my obsessive, intrusive thoughts but the need to check things sort of disappeared. Was it a worthy trade-off? I don't know. Smoking was the only thing available to me. It sped up my progress in therapy. It helped me become more insightful. But now it's slowing me down. The sudden withdrawal of the weed caused damage to me—I get at least one symptom of psychosis when I'm anxious.

Repeatedly stopping smoking cold turkey and restarting caused me to get too excited by girls. I felt as though I was getting more and more deeply into it, like a bad episode— like I am tripping. The Zyprexa helps but I'm so obsessional in my head. I get caught up in worrying about what damage the weed did to me.

Dr. M says the weed didn't do any permanent damage. Then how does one explain the psychotic symptoms that started about three months after I restarted smoking?

March 2004

My neurologist started me on Trileptal to help me stop smoking. I'm feeling nervous. I'm feeling the beginning of a tension headache. I have mild urges to check things. The stress headache is kicking in late this afternoon. I feel my throat starting to hurt. I think that going off the weed is lowering my immune system. It's like the time when I first started smoking. It also lowered my immune system. I used Imitrex nasal spray. It seems to have helped with my tension headache. A little time has passed and the tension headache is coming back. I'm feeling an increase in urges to check things. I had to smoke weed.

April 26, 2004

I feel very unfocused. My mind feels blank—empty of thoughts or ideas. When I'm in conversations with people, I have no ideas to express. It's impossible to organize my thoughts. I have nothing to say to people. I wish life would come to an end.

May 10, 2004

I went to see the healer, Jake.

May 17, 2004

I'm feeling a little bit better today. I'm not suffering mentally. Before I went on Zyprexa, I would think that if I were to walk in front of a car and get hit, it's meant to be. Now I'm on Zyprexa and those thoughts stopped. They seem to be replaced by obsessive thoughts about whether there is a God in the world. Is it significant when something good happens? For instance, right when I walked into the drug store, the pharmacist called my name—perfect timing. I start thinking that it's a power from up above.

June 6, 2004

I don't care to live. I am happy that since I saw the healer, Jake, I've been able to take just 5 mg of Zyprexa without having extremely painful, psychotic episodes. I'm worried that it's not going to last and that just makes me not want to live anymore. I have so little to say to people.

June 8, 2004

I am feeling depressed, irritable and having tension headaches. I don't feel like drumming because I'm feeling weak. I'm feeling that scared or nervous feeling in my stomach. When I went to the library, just thinking about returning books was overwhelming me and I didn't take out any books. I'm feeling mentally blank—nothing to say.

June 12, 2004- August 2004

Days after I saw Jake, I was feeling clearer than usual. I had more things to say to people and was articulate when speaking with Dr. M. about how smoking marijuana fucked up my brain. That didn't last long. Now I am not thinking clearly. I can't think about how stopping the marijuana cold turkey messed me up.

It's been two months without smoking weed and I am now able to finish my sentences. I can drum because I am not in a vegetative state. Since I've seen Jake, my mental suffering lessened to the point where I am able to go down to 5 mg of Zyprexa. At this moment, though, it's harder to gather my thoughts in my own head than it has been for the past week, even more so when I am in other's company. I had to increase the amount of Zyprexa I was taking because I was getting stress headaches and getting overwhelmed by everything. Now that I am up to 10 mg of Zyprexa, I am not having stress headaches. ` Since I've seen Jake, I have not been afraid to play the drums.

June 17, 2004

Some parts of the trip to Israel were nice, but a lot of the time there I was miserable. I couldn't remember most of the people's names. I couldn't speak to people that I liked. I was embarrassed that I couldn't remember what they did. I also had nothing to say to them. I already had a hard time remembering names before I started smoking weed. Since I stopped smoking cold, it's close to impossible. Numerous times on the trip I was feeling suicidal because of the tease of feeling better from Jake. It lasted for a while and now it's gone. Unless it's in the form of music, I don't have the ability to absorb information, specifically in word format. It might possibly be easier to remember beats now than before I had chronic disorganized thinking and the feeling of being blank. I feel dumber with words and smarter with beats.

June 18, 2004

All I keep thinking about is that there will be a terrorist attack and hoping there will be one soon. I'm feeling overwhelmed thinking about doing things. I'm having a bad headache. I feel overwhelmed thinking about practicing to read drum notes and in general, studying beats by heart. I don't have anything to say to my friends. Life sucks shit. I drank a lot of liquor last night to try to numb the pain. It hurts to experience the damage done from smoking weed; not being able to organize my thoughts and empty of thoughts. The only thoughts that I do have is whether there is a God in the world and if and when there will be a terrorist attack.

August 8, 2004

I am feeling weak every day now. I can barely drum. The only thing that stops me from killing myself is that I think there will be an attack and a big one at that. Otherwise, I would probably kill myself. Maybe I'll do it anyways. What kind of a fucked up world is this? First, I am dealt a shitty hand and given a problem that is way over my head to deal with. Then, this psychic guy comes along and gives me relief from my symptoms for a week or two. I was feeling energetic, not feeling overwhelmed by everything, not feeling weak, and now I'm feeling all of the above. I am very embarrassed that I went to my older brother's house and started speaking to him about how I don't believe there is a God in the world. I have totally lost my mind.

August 11, 2004

I wasn't feeling weak today. I was able to drum to most of the songs I played to, even Metallica. I played for over an hour without feeling overwhelmed that it might disturb others. I also know that if I don't drum, I start doubting whether I can drum or not. The only problem is, since I feel like I have something to live for, I start worrying that there might be a terrorist attack and I don't want it to happen. My mind is fucked. I can't remember names. All I can remember is drum beats. I start thinking about how things kind of worked out for me: Me finding my neurologist and that he was able to get me off the weed. Maybe God does work through us in some way. I've come so far with playing the drums, I couldn't have stayed in a vegetative state. It's as though the effort I put in to succeed encouraged God to offer me help, though, maybe a little too late. I don't know what's wrong with me. I start to think that the weed was so dangerous to me but I can't even think about what it actually did. I'm blocked. The same way I was fixed on telling Dr. M. how the weed fucked up my mind, I get fixed on whether or not I should discuss my anger in therapy. Dr. M. takes that as a sign that I really should be discussing my anger and about how exaggerated it is.

August 17, 2004

I'm beginning to think again that there will probably be an attack on New York this coming Republican convention. That would be a needed distraction from this hell. My doubts are driving me nuts. If one day I don't play the drums well, I start doubting whether I can play at all and I feel down the whole day—like I have nothing to live for. I'm not feeling so agitated at people and I am overall in a better mood and I am not feeling as blank. I can speak to people, somewhat. I am not sure why at times I doubt the extent of the damage the weed did to me. Maybe it is anxiety, similar to when I doubt whether I'm good at playing the drums if I don't drum well all the time.

August 20, 2004

I feel horrible today. I feel agitated by everything. I am very angry. I have gone into this psychotic state where the only thing I can speak about is how wrong it is for people to have kids. Also, I'm just hoping there will be a terrorist attack. I just want to kill myself. Everything happened to me at the wrong times. If only I would have met Jake before I got into smoking weed (which I partly had to do since I would just get overwhelmed too easily). When I couldn't drum anymore I had nothing. Maybe if Jake had suggested back then that I take the vitamins and had healed me with his hands, I might have avoided ruining my mind. I don't know if my feeling down today has something to do with the beer drinking I did last night. I couldn't drum well today. I didn't even want to drum because I got sucked into this negative perception that I have about life and how it's cursed.

August 28, 2004

I wasn't feeling very agitated at the beginning of the day. I was able to be humorous. Later, I became agitated with obsessively worrying. This is going on too many days in a row. I am ready to end this shit. My mind is driving me nuts because I told my brother that I don't want his friend to come over and then I was overridden with guilt. In all this misery, I did drum well for half an hour. So, I feel a little better. I am not thinking clearly about why I told my brother he can't bring his friend over to drum and whether the excuse I told him was good enough. My excuse was that I didn't feel comfortable with him drumming and I keep thinking about that in constant pain. I am damned if he does come over and play because I will feel agitated and upset that my brother chooses his friend to drum with him over me. I also don't like people touching my stuff. However, if he doesn't come over, I'll feel guilty. I can't win. Life sucks!

September 3, 2004

I am feeling obsessional with my thoughts about terrorist attacks and feeling an unsettled feeling of checking things. For example, my brother's car was parked close to my mother's car, so I felt the need to move it. I didn't, though, and I felt very unsettled about it. My head is hurting and I am feeling more depressed tonight. I told my mother, "What are you doing sending me to school and having me be abused in front of your eyes?" My mother was complaining that people in the family don't respect each other, but she wasn't respecting me by not acknowledging my pain. Now I feel guilty that I said that. I am so confused. It's hard to make conversation even with my family. I drank three Beers and I was talking with my friend and

I really didn't have much to say. So, I blurted a line from a movie, "Did you get it on with my sister?" I don't know what is with my mind. I guess my mind is not as blank as it was before I saw Jake, but it's still pretty bad. It's really sad that the only way I can communicate to people is saying phrases from movies that I remember.

September 4, 2004

Just the thought of doing anything like shopping feels too much. I should speak to my neurologist to see if there's a medicine for that and also for my mind having lack of thought.

September 6, 2004

The thought of getting a haircut is too much for me. Life is not getting better with me feeling overwhelmed by everything.

September 7, 2004

I am feeling weak and overwhelmed. Just thinking about getting a prescription filled feels too much. I'm feeling very agitated. I couldn't drum well. I was feeling very nervous to drum. At night, I am not agitated or overwhelmed. I'm not feeling that scary feeling in the stomach. I have a headache at night. It's a tension headache. I was hoping there would be an attack on the US.

September 9, 2004

I am feeling weak again. Though, I'm not feeling as overwhelmed with thinking about things I have to do. There's something really wrong with my brain. I feel almost paralyzed when it comes to wanting to communicate with people. My friends complain that I'm so quiet. I have no words to say. I've been severely damaged. I am feeling overwhelmed with the idea of drumming but I feel weak so I won't drum anyway. I am not feeling agitated. Instead, I am feeling weak every day now.

September 12, 2004

I am not feeling agitated right now. I am, however, feeling an increase of the urge to check things. An unsettling feeling overcomes me that I didn't do something correctly and I start doubting. Physically, I'm feeling only a little weak. I was even able to bike around the park. I can't feel good about exercising because I start doubting that I exercised correctly— I can't prove to myself that I did. Something is very wrong with my brain and I can't make sense out of what people are saying. I feel confused, especially when I consume alcohol. The onset of headaches came later today. I'm starting to feel more nervous around my family.

September 13, 2004

I feel like something bad is going to happen to the country. This is because things in my life didn't quite work out the way I'd like, like having a problem I can't deal with. It's way too much to deal with. At least I am not feeling weak but my mind is not working too well in regards to trying to understand things. I'm unsure if it's due to my learning disability but I can't comprehend the exercises my younger brother was showing me. I'm experiencing an increase in moodiness at night. I was feeling agitated with my older brother because he was asking me what exercises I want to do and if I have weights. I just don't see the point in making conversation if he's not going to remember this conversation. Maybe he will. When I am trying to think things through, I use up so much energy trying to understand it that I get a headache and I don't achieve understanding.

September 16, 2004

I am feeling a bit of a tension headache. After taking the clonazepam, I feel less anxious and less agitated. It only gets a little bit easier to engage in conversations, but barely. I don't think anybody has a right to have kids or to inflict suffering on to others. The pain that can be experienced is infinite. There can be so much pain physically and emotionally. It's wrong to have kids. For the sake of the unfortunate people that end up suffering, it isn't right to take a chance of having kids, especially since life is unpredictable. Circumstances can change, like the future that's in store resulting from terrorism. I hope I die from a rare brain disease. I just want to die. I might as well suffer with a purpose. There is no limit to how much a person can suffer in a lifetime. These people did nothing wrong. There is no point to this suffering or this world in general.

September 18, 2004

I am worrying that I'm going to feel miserable again because I told my sister that God is the only one not doing his job in the world. But with me it seems me having contact with my neurologist, Jake and Elena was from God. So, how can I say that? I feel nervous to drum. When I get nervous while drumming, I slow down. I'm not going to succeed in the drumming business if I can't play in front of people. I have to get an electric drum set to reduce the loudness of the sound. I am feeling very nervous. I am trying to avoid my older brother for I fear he is going to ask me why I drummed.

September 19, 2004

I feel like I really lost my mind with feeling sure that one day there will be a terrorist attack. This world happened by chance. Though, today I am not so sure there will be attack—I'm thinking maybe part of this world is by chance and some not. Regarding myself: I feel totally unorganized. I can't think clearly. I can't express any of my opinions because I don't have one, except that people ought not to have kids. Even that I am not sure about. I feel sure there'll be a terrorist attack when things are not going well for me.

September 20, 2004

The drums didn't sound too loud today but I wasn't on beat a hundred percent of the time. It wasn't that great. My thoughts are obsessed with worrying if I can ever play on beat. My mood keeps flip-flopping back and forth. As soon as I am reminded that I didn't play good today, I feel horrible. I wasn't totally in control with the drums but I feel I did alright with the music I was playing with Jon and my dad. I am now feeling sure that there will be a terrorist attack, after my sister asked me what Armageddon is. I was fucked, so this world must be fucked. But I'll keep flip-flopping back and forth like I do with the idea whether there is a God in the world or not. My mind is gone. I feel very unfocused today about where I stand with my beliefs about myself and the world. I have a lot of trouble expressing myself.

September 21, 2004

I was feeling overwhelmed because my shades from my windows fell down. I felt it was too much. I was suffering so much that I wouldn't mind dying or being a victim of a terrorist attack and get killed. I can't really do anything. I go through so much pain if I have tasks to do. Unfocused, I can't express myself to people. I was talking with my little sister and explained to her the things that happen in the world are random and some of them aren't. I wasn't clear explaining about what it would mean if some of this world was not an accident.

September 24, 2004

I am feeling weak again today and couldn't really do anything. I was able to drum to some songs. I have this fear of getting into the music because then it might appear like I'm good at it. For example, moving or being animated with the music. Only sometimes am I not afraid to get into the music when I'm being observed. There are two reasons why I get afraid: 1. if I get into it, I might be disturbing others more than I would if I didn't get into it. 2. I am afraid of receiving compliments that I play well, so I try not to look too good.

I am fed up with life. I feel so confused after my brother told me that on one specific day in the year, I shouldn't turn on the television. I told him Yom Kippur is bullshit. Now my thought patterns regarding the possibility of a terrorist attack occurring have returned. If there is a God in the world, how could he have allowed all this shit to happen to an innocent little boy since high school? I guess I am conflicted whether I should keep the holidays. Maybe this conflict is contributing to why I'm not thinking clearly anymore. Earlier today I was thinking more clearly than I was in a long time. The end result of smoking has made me not think clearly. I can't stand that I doubt whether I'm good at the drums. My mind is fucked. I love God, sick fuck.

September 25, 2004

Life sucks. I am feeling weak and too afraid to drum. I am worrying that since I didn't keep Yom Kippur, bad things will happen to me. Maybe God is out to make my life as miserable as possible.

September 28 2004

I am feeling weak today. I was able to drum a little but got tired quickly. I'm not feeling weak late in the afternoon. I was able to express myself to my father better than I have in the past. But, I still feel that there is something wrong with my brain, especially when I'm anxious. All my thoughts become disorganized. For instance, I was looking forward to perhaps going to this Birthright gathering and maybe meet girls. I get so excited and that makes it harder to express myself in the company of others.

October 3, 2004

I felt empty of ideas to express to people at this party I went to tonight. I saw some girls. I just don't have anything to say and I get nervous. This makes it even harder to organize my thoughts.

October 15, 2004

How can I come to accept my problems when my problem is that I can't make sense of the words people say to me? The Zyprexa is not helping with my unclear thoughts. The damage done by the weed seems to be permanent. The only thing Jake seems to have given me was the temporary relief of thinking clearly for a couple of days.

October 19, 2004

I was able to drum but not quite on beat this afternoon. Later in the afternoon I was feeling suicidal. I can't drum the way my older brother wants me to drum, to get into the music and be relaxed. I just am feeling stubborn again. I'm angry that I've had to go through so much pain throughout my life and I want to end this frustration and pain just to spite my parents. I want to take my life.

I don't really want to take responsibility for this shitty life; like making a schedule for myself as my friend suggested. This fantasy that I have about killing myself is a place of comfort and I enjoy being there. I was actually able to sit in one place in my older brother's room and watch movies while getting into them without feeling too fidgety.

I was feeling agitated at my family, not as much as in the past, but I was feeling quite unhappy. Later in the afternoon in my pissed off mood, I played the drums on beat with the music. I know that I don't look like I am into it; at least not like the way my brother wants me to play. When I drum, I mimic what other drummers are doing, and I am not putting emotion into it—it looks dead. That's what's missing from my drumming. I am also afraid to put life into it because I'm afraid of what I'll look like. For instance, when Charles puts life into his drumming, it looks weird. I'm afraid I'll look weird. Also, the fear of disturbing others stops me from getting fully into the music.

October 31, 2004

I'm not feeling weak. I was feeling really nervous to play the drums this afternoon. I did it anyway only because I played with my brother. I took my bike to get a haircut. The barber cut my hair too short in the front and you were able to see the ridges on my head. I feel so embarrassed and angry that this happened to me. Seeing the ridges reminded me how badly I feel that I had to get into smoking and hurt myself. I was hoping that there would be a terrorist attack that would end my life. I came home and felt like shit. Later in the afternoon, I had a sudden change of mood. I was feeling happier and less nervous. I was able to drum and get into it. I felt good that I drummed well and didn't have to drink liquor or beer.

November 1, 2004

I wasn't feeling too nervous to play the drums today. I wasn't feeling weak. I drummed okay. It annoyed me so much when Brad came over here and played the drums. He moved them and I felt unsettled. Before he played, I told my father that he will have to play it in the exact placing it's in. My father said he won't be able to play it the way it is so I said that's too bad. I felt angry because my father always wants to enjoy himself at my expense. I feel that he thinks his pleasures are more important than my emotional health. For instance, when I couldn't play the drums, Brad would come over and it would kill me to hear him play on my drum set. It hurt so badly. I had to get into smoking and it caused me harm. It would've been a lot easier for me if he wouldn't play and maybe I would've been able to tolerate my inability to play the drums better and wouldn't have had to be self-destructive.

Of course, back then, I didn't have the guts to tell my father that Brad shouldn't play. Today I do. Eventually, the anger faded and I was feeling guilty that I didn't want him to play. I kept on thinking about it. Later at night, after I put the drums back into its place, I was jamming with my brother. I didn't really want to but he insisted. My sister got angry and now

I'm obsessing about that. It just doesn't end. My thoughts are so intrusive.

November 10, 2004

I feel overwhelmed. I decided to buy a jukebox from a friend and one of his settings makes the music sound distorted. I couldn't drum well today at all. I can't drum to songs I don't know the exact drumming to. I couldn't drum well to the songs I knew. I will never become a drummer. I just get easily overwhelmed maybe even easier now because I'm down on my Zyprexa. I'm feeling a little weak today.

I'm getting into my thoughts of whether there is a God in the world and that a big attack will eventually happen and I just imagine how shocked people would be when they believed so strongly that there is a God and it turns out there isn't. I've really had it with this life. It sucks shit. Probably the same thing that happened to allow Elena's healing to occur and diminish will happen with Jake's healing. I cried thinking about all the pain I've gone through and go through and will have to go through. If there is a God in the world, he doesn't care that much about his creation. He supposedly gives the land of Israel to the Jews and then he wants us to fight it over with the Arab's. I'm having a tension headache. It's hard to appreciate the songs when I'm listening to my friend's jukebox. I keep focusing on a distorted sound to see if it's there and not the song itself.

November 14, 2004

I went to a bar last night with a friend and I drank a lot. I felt like I couldn't explain things to people. I was trying to explain to a drummer how I got into copying other drummers and how I can't seem to tap into my own creativity. I'm feeling a little confused today, definitely not as bad as the last times I've drank before I saw the healer, Jake. I am not feeling depressed but I am having intrusive thoughts—doubting that I can even drum because I didn't practice today. I'm not feeling agitated. I did start having bad headaches later in the day. I feel a little down because my doubts of whether I am a good drummer take away from me feeling proud by how far I've gotten.

November 21, 2004

I was feeling agitated earlier in the day but later in the day I was feeling less agitated. Although, the thought of Brad coming over gets on my nerves but it's not as bad as yesterday. My obsessions over whether I will be able to play the drums if my drum set is moved are not as bad. I'm having clarity in thought today and I was able to drum well today even in front of my brother's friend. I'm feeling happier especially since I'm progressing at the drums.

November 22, 2004

I am feeling a lot better today; not agitated and no tension headaches. I wasn't really drumming well at the beginning of the day because I was only feeling tired not weak.

I drummed with Jon and my dad. I drummed well since I was able to relax. My mother was watching me play. When my father and Jon were talking, I was trying to follow. Jon was talking about psychological aspects. I feel that all of the work with Dr. M is missing. I don't know where I stand with my beliefs. The one thing I know I stand for is that I don't blame evil people for the bad they do because they don't have much of a choice. I shared my belief with Jon but he feels people do have choice as long as they are not retarded. I don't know if I sound a little off with that belief.

I do know that I couldn't control myself with bothering my sister or my mother. I still have trouble not bothering her. I have somewhat of a choice whether to do it or not more than five years ago. I don't think evil people have a choice until they have reached a certain point with some type of therapy but until then, their urge is too strong.

November 24, 2004

I am feeling scared that Jake's healing will stop since God is evil, I'm afraid that he will tease me. I feel like probably girls outnumber guys by 5 to 1. It's like having a Holocaust except the creator wants it to be known that he is the one behind the evil.

November 27, 2004

I went to a bar with my friend, Mo. I had three Long Island ice teas. I got very drunk and now I feel flu-like symptoms. I feel weak. I am not feeling as confused as after the previous times I drank. I can't drum. I feel depressed. I want to die already. I'm thinking about World War III. I'm glad man invented nuclear weapons and will destroy everybody's life because there is too much suffering in this world. For the sake of people suffering in this world, it should be destroyed. There is no reason for pain. Just because some people enjoy themselves, it doesn't mean that life should continue. I would rather know that suffering will end. There's no reason for this life. It is all about sex. It's an evil creator we are dealing with if there is one.

November 30, 2004

I was thinking about how it's good that my mother had miscarriages so she didn't bring more suffering into this world. Although not everyone in the family suffers, I do think a lot of the family is disturbed and suffers a lot. I went through so fucking much, it's ridiculous. At least I do feel it's a little easier to find words to express myself.

December 3, 2004

I am having very bad intrusive thoughts about when my father's friends come over and move my drum set. I can't even look forward to the new house where I can drum almost any time because I think about my drum set being moved. The room it will be in will be sound proof. I feel like it gets ruined and I won't be able to get it back to its original place and drum well. I am feeling really agitated at everyone—I don't feel that I have anything to look forward to. I was so upset that I drummed to Evanescence even though it disturbs the family. I just didn't care. I drummed alright, but wasn't able to do anything fast; only the simple beats they do on the record. I am feeling unclear. I am feeling very depressed at night. I couldn't say a word to anyone and I really wanted to end this stupid life. This feeling was triggered from the thought that my drum set will be moved in the future. So, I had five shot glasses of liquor. I started feeling numb all over my body but it only lasted an hour. I was listening to Metallica on my loudspeaker because Mo was here. I didn't care if my family would hear it, especially since my mother said earlier that the reason she sent me to yeshiva is because that's what God wanted.

December 15, 2004

I feel a little drunk. I drank three beers and four shots of scotch. I don't feel more confused because of it. I do feel very relaxed and dizzy. When my brother penalized me for not working, I was able to tell him that if it weren't for me and my younger brother clearing out the new house, we wouldn't be anywhere near building it up. I'm kind of sick of music so I didn't really drum today. I did for a little but I started feeling tired after ten minutes. I feel hyped after drinking all that stuff.

December 17 2004

I was feeling very agitated all day. I didn't feel like speaking to anyone. This evening I was feeling so agitated I didn't really say a word at the table. The agitation extended even to Mo. I am feeling really miserable and weak. Tonight I am feeling less agitated. I am better able to express myself. My obsessive thoughts are bad. I'm continuously thinking about the ridges on my head and that it will result in death with my skull sinking in and squashing my brain. I was trying to tell myself not to think about it because after all I've been through, why should I put myself through more?

December 21, 2004

I drank four beers. The high didn't last long. The thoughts I was having while I was high listening to Toni Braxton repeatedly were that a nuclear attack is likely to happen soon. That makes me feel that all the learning I've done with the drum and bass is all in vain. These thoughts about a terrorist attack are so distressing, but I keep entertaining them. I was feeling very nervous when listening to my mother speak on the radio imagining what will happen if I'm in front of an audience. I'm feeling nervous around everybody. When will this hell end? Then I think about how I could have remained in a vegetative state just like that other patient. So, I can't complain about how tough life is. Not only that, but the brain-damage that was caused from the abrupt stop to smoking has somewhat gone away. Now, I feel happy to be able to drum, learn the bass and play the piano. I could've been left being unable to do anything.

December 23, 2004

It seems I have really gotten help from Jake with my mind. I have my mind back. I actually have things to say to people. It's not blank—like nothing is on my mind. I can come up with the words I want to express to people to make conversation. I'm not a mute anymore. I hope it lasts. It seems everything else has lasted.

I can't sleep at night. My mind keeps on running. It doesn't shut down. Something that was caused from the healing is having difficulty sleeping and then getting sick because my immunity gets low. Then, I start having difficulty expressing myself, feeling confused, agitated and depressed. I'm feeling too excited about getting better with my emotional health and with music.

December 30, 2004

I was really upset to hear that Charles was yelling at my father about my drum set being not good and sounded like cardboard. He said that he will have to start playing in his studio, which I wouldn't mind. If he can't stand the way I tune the drums then, fuck him! But it was bothering me a lot. When he came over tonight, I felt this tension between Charles and me which made me feel like I wasn't good at the drums. So, I went to the gym to keep my mind off of it and it worked. I was feeling so down because of what Charles said that I wanted to end this shitty life and started thinking about a potential attack. I'm worried that drinking while taking medications may cause damage to the brain. I have to limit how and when I drink.

January 12, 2005

I feel little by little I am more able to absorb information that I gather from movies, books and conversations with others. Jake has really helped me a lot. When I am watching a movie, my mind doesn't wander to the only thought I would have. Thoughts of whether there is a God in the world or if there's a path for everyone. I'm able to get involved in the movie and get into what they're saying. Jake fixed whatever part of the brain that was damaged from the smoking or stopping of it cold. I feel clarity in thought. It almost feels like the way it was before the damage happened. I'm not quite there yet. Maybe I will someday. I also don't get overwhelmed as frequently as before. I'm taking now 2.5 mg of Zyprexa. Taking out books from the library doesn't overwhelm me too much but a mess that I'd have to clean up would. My tolerance for anxiety is a little higher.

January 15, 2005

From what I remember, I started having severe psychotic episodes which caused me complete lack of control over my thoughts and would come as waves of attack. At times I was free. I also had an extremely abnormal need for girls. I would go off into these episodes of feeling the desire or excitement and it would keep on getting more and more intense.

Eventually, I would come out of the attack. So Dr. M. referred me to a psychiatrist at this time. I was also speaking to Elena. She had an effect on these episodes. At first, the episodes were getting worse then it slowly became better. It saddens me to think of all the sufferers out there specifically those that have gotten into smoking marijuana and were left in a vegetative state—not being able to say anything to anyone, just feeling embarrassed and scared that it will remain this way. Fortunately for me, when I started smoking again I came out of the state but I did cause brain damage. Damage which could have been permanent but thanks to Jake, my brain has become less damaged and the confused thinking will hopefully get better. The intense mental suffering which in no doubt reached psychotic levels is lessened significantly even on 2.5 mg of Zyprexa. The heightened sexual need for girls has lessened significantly. Even my obsessive thoughts have lessened but it is still intrusive. The fear if I miss a day of practicing the drums, that I'll lose technique, has also lessoned.

January 19, 2005

It's a little scary to think about the different religions that claim to be God's chosen one. The idea that Jews are God chosen people is bullshit. The creator probably gave the information across to somebody just to stir a fight throughout time. One of the reasons for creation is war. What makes good people any better than bad people? Who says good is chosen over evil by a creator. They are just supposed to fight. It's not right for people who are unfortunate and do evil things to not only be somewhat possessed but to be mocked for it. That's double the suffering—added insult to injury. When I bothered my little sister, not only was I suffering greatly emotionally, which of course led me to not have much control over my actions, but I had to suffer with having pointed fingers at me insinuating I'm bad. I couldn't help myself. How many sick people out there can't help but let their emotions out on someone through murdering or raping? I bet they don't even have a choice to do it or not. I know I didn't when I bothered my little sister. Even when I knew I would be yelled at or hit for doing it, I did it anyway. This is truly hell for a lot people. It's the same thing with gays. They don't choose to be that way. When someone asks me if a person killed someone in your family, would I want that person to receive punishment? I say yes. He should be responsible for his actions. Maybe he won't do it again or he should be forced to seek help and be supervised doing so.

January 28, 2005

    I felt really agitated when I came home from group therapy and my family was asking me about it and I couldn't speak because of it. At night, I'm feeling less agitated but I was feeling nervous around my father. In the support group, I was anticipating that when talking in front of the group my mind would go blank. It sort of did. But when I spoke, I was clearer than I thought I'd be. I was in a fairly good mood. Then I was speaking to my sister about her rash that she has all over her body and she was saying that she'll just let it get worse until she dies. She says she has nothing in her life worth living for. After that conversation, I was feeling really depressed. As much as I want to have understanding to others' pain, I shouldn't do it while I'm feeling good because it just brings me down.

January 31, 2005

I am not feeling agitated. I am feeling unclear with my thoughts. Now I'm feeling really upset that the only thing I can speak about is how random this world seems to be. I brought it up as my older sister said, "I don't know what God wants from me". I don't know if my thoughts sound sort of psychotic since the smoking. I should try to keep it to myself even though they make sense to me; thoughts about whether there's a God in the world and evil people shouldn't be considered bad. I don't know what to do about the support group I'm attending. These people have come out of jail. Not all of them did, but many have. I'm so afraid of telling the person in charge that I don't want to come back. I feel overwhelmed just going. I feel even more overwhelmed to say I don't want to attend anymore. Maybe I'll just not go. The thought of me going to this support group and meet people—that God will set up an encounter with a girl or friend is false. I'm not being guided by God to go to this program. It really doesn't seem like my crowd. I started thinking in this spiritual way since the marijuana use. But, I have met some people like Jake, Elena, and my neurologist, and they all have helped me, somewhat. If there is no guidance from up above, then how does anything work out? My life hasn't worked out until things were really hopeless. So, I tried killing myself by smoking and damaging my lungs—engaging in my self-destructive tendencies— which caused me to go into a vegetative state. I came out of it when I restarted smoking. I was being caused permanent damage until I got a hold of my neurologist and Jake. I find that for anything to really work out there has to be a supreme being to let it happen. For some reason, I've been allowed somewhat of a recovery. I contribute my recovery to maintain my ability to drum and to keep other people's minds off of their suffering. But, when my wrists start to hurt from the drumming, it shoots holes in that theory.

February 2, 2005

I felt pretty clear what I have to work on with Dr. M. I need to develop skills to deal with the fear I have of others' anger. It makes it very hard to stick up for myself in fear of upsetting the other person. I need to work on my poor tolerance with anxiety in general. It's not always bad. I feel guilty about bothering my little sister all my life since she was born. I mentioned to my mother I bought her a gift and my mother said that my little sister and I are very close. I added, "Really close since she was born". My mother said, "Boy did you bother her a lot". She said I ruined her life.

February 6, 2005

I am worried about going down on the Trileptal and that it will cause an increase in my need to check things. It may also cause me to go into a vegetative state and maybe get nightmares. I don't really feel like I can look forward to anything. Jake's healing might not last. I am thinking that since I don't feel there is a purpose to my existence that I shouldn't exist. But since when does there have to be a purpose in order to exist? Why not just live? I started having these thoughts yesterday while speaking about this with Mo.

February 16, 2005

My thoughts are a lot more focused. I've been thinking about how we come from nothing which is atoms to human beings. I don't feel it's possible that all of these atoms, dust particles formed itself into such organized intelligent forms of life by accident. Some higher power must have made it possible. I think that my life got some help from a supreme being. Things miraculously were fixed from the damage the weed did to me. I'm almost symptom free. It's almost the way it was before I started smoking. I am not as obsessive with my thoughts or with checking things. It feels to me that there is a higher power and it will intervene when there is a crisis, for me an internal crisis. God is not so kind but there is obviously a touch of good in him. There is a setup with the universe with Earth having a gravitational pull. The ingredients for life to be able to form exist. That doesn't mean that God creates everything that exists. Sometimes, he does put his thought into human existence but I think he leaves a lot of it to chance.

February 21, 2005

I stopped taking Zyprexa today. I hurt my right ankle and both of my wrists from playing drums, piano and a little bass guitar. It bothers me I feel so emotionally far apart from my parent's—like I don't know them. I can't even appreciate being loved because it doesn't mean anything to me. It's sad but true. I can't communicate with my mother because what I have to say is usually negative and about wanting to die. There is no common ground in relating except musically. I don't trust my mother enough to tell her private things because I feel she can't keep certain things private. I don't know if my mother is real to me all the time and I don't know if my father loves me. Though, maybe he cares about me, somewhat. I was feeling nervous in front of my entire family, even my little sister. I was especially nervous when I was telling her that I'm emotionally numb because of what I've been through and she wanted me to give her eye contact.

March 9, 2005

I discussed with Dr. M. of my distrust in him because of how therapy made me worse and how I'm not willing to get into my feelings for the fear of them blowing up. Dr. M. asked me how I feel about him not helping me. I said that I'm upset but I don't feel in touch with the anger. He's trying to get me in touch with my feelings not just with anger, but feelings of attachment with my friends and family. I strongly believe that smoking marijuana has taken that away from me for good. I don't think I can retrieve that.

March 14, 2005

My thoughts are very unpleasant. I'm thinking that there will be an attack soon because of the recent intercepted call from Bin Laden to another terrorist to attack in the US. My thoughts are so depressive. I can't control them. Even with some good things happening to me, like getting off the Zyprexa without any significant collapse in my thinking capacity, I just get sucked into this negative reality.

March 23, 2005

I went to see my new therapist. I don't know what to do. If I am to see my new therapist then I have to discontinue with Dr. M. and we just started focusing more on a behavioral approach to my problems. I'm afraid I'll hurt him by choosing the new therapist over Dr. M. But the new therapist is free. I'm still concerned about Dr. M. making things worse for me. I cried for a minute thinking of leaving Dr.M. We've been through a lot together.

March 29, 2005

I'm sick of this stupid life. I can't express myself freely; for example, the situation at the Gym. I wanted to cancel my membership but they said that I can't. Later on, the guy told me he will freeze my account for the next two months. I didn't put up much of a fight. I can't accept myself being a wuss. I get very nervous when love is expressed to me. That might be because it's embarrassing for me not to be able to connect to whoever is expressing love and I'm embarrassed of feeling uncomfortable. There is a vulnerability involved with me letting myself be taken over by emotions of love. Maybe I don't want to make myself vulnerable and feel a loss of control.

April 19, 2005

I downloaded a lot of songs from a friend of mine. When I came home, I asked my older brother if he could download a disk so that I could copy music onto my jukebox. He asked me if I have ever downloaded things on the computer. I said yes. He was so angry he said he doesn't want me using his computer if I don't know how to use it. Now I'm feeling guilty that I messed up the computer by downloading things and I feel afraid of him getting angry at me in the future.

May 9, 2005

I drummed a little using my left foot and hurt it. Now both of my ankles hurt. Great. After watching this movie last night about war in Israel against Christians and Muslims, it got me thinking that there is no individual plan for each of us. Our existence is totally dependent on each other whether we hurt or kill each other. There is no higher power, it seems, that really protects us. Sometimes a miracle can happen, but mostly it seems that people are the ones in control, not God. All I know is that I've went through so much emotional pain. I am very against bringing new life into this world. Not only can there be endless emotional suffering but also physical. It's ridiculous of course. There can be a significant amount of pleasure but I don't care. I won't do unto an unborn child what I didn't want to be done to myself. And even if there is a chance the child could have a fairly decent life, I'm not taking that chance. After all, I am leaving it to chance. There isn't thought put into what's going to happen. It's random which sperm cell will make it to the mother's egg. At which point, anything could go wrong while being in the mother's uterus. Then there's bringing it into this fucked up world. My life doesn't have a path.

May 11, 2005

I bumped into an old friend who had also been seeing Dr. M. He seems to be doing fine. He's off all of his meds. I saw him work behind the register and he seems to know what he's doing. His brain seems to be functioning. That makes me jealous. I was feeling depressed after I saw my new therapist. I couldn't take life anymore. I was so tired in session that I couldn't think. I was suffering mentally from feeling weird that I'm seeing two therapists and feeling guilty that it's upsetting the new therapist. The clinic does not allow it and it seems to bother him because it's against the policy. The new therapist may have been trying to use reverse psychology on me by telling me, "Why engage in life if it has no meaning or purpose?" (I wish I would have told him at the time, "Do I have a choice to engage or not?")

May 13, 2005

My father was trying to give over something from what he learned in his religious studies and I disagreed with him. I didn't even wait until he was finished speaking. I'm filled with so much anger about how I feel that this world is bullshit and pointless. So, when he says that God wants us to get closer to him, I tell him that he wants to push us away by putting us through so much shit. I feel that I had a kind of trade off with my mental pain being greatly alleviated from the healing Jake has done with me being more physically fragile with my wrists and ankles. My mind is functioning now. I appreciate talking with people and expressing my views and it feels fairly focused.

May 24, 2005

My older brother came home from working at the new house. He found me watching TV. He was so angry that I'm not helping out with the house. I told him that the doctor doesn't allow me to do that work because I'm in pain. He mocked, "Doctor", and chuckled.

May 27, 2005

My new therapist feels that if a patient is driven to suicidal behaviors due to the therapy which brought him in touch with his emotions, then the therapy was improperly done. It's possible if I had met with this new therapist much earlier I wouldn't have had my emotions blown up to such an extent.

May 29, 2005

When Mo came over to drum, it triggered a very deep depression. I went to my younger brother's room and listened to the Chopin CD my mother bought me for my birthday and cried. I was going through so much pain for a few hours. Now I am not as depressed. My new therapist feels that psychotherapy, when used for anger, is not good because it never ends; you never stop feeling anger by continuing to explore it. This is what seemed to be happening in my case. I would talk about my feelings and my anger became more intense as the years went by. He also said that studies show it is more likely for patients to commit suicide if they used the psychodynamic approach to psychotherapy. He continued on to say that with behavioral therapy, the goal is not to intensify the feelings by talking about what happened in the past. In fact, he says he doesn't want to know what happened to me. He will just deal with the here and now symptoms. But what if the emotions really are intense inside and you're not in touch with them? Well, it seems you're doomed either way. Either you'll suffer with psychosomatic symptoms as well as severe depression from not getting the repressed emotions to the surface. Or, if you do get it to the surface, then you can eventually go into a state of madness and there will never be an end to your anger. You won't come to terms with it and eventually you'll let it out on yourself by harming yourself or ultimately killing yourself.

With regard to my poor anxiety tolerance, talking didn't help me. Medications helped me a little bit. I had to keep increasing the Zoloft because I was experiencing my feelings more and more intensely and having worse headaches. With Dr. M., I got my feelings to the surface and needed a refuge place and had suicidal fantasies in my state of anger. That was my escape. Maybe, if I had met this new therapist, we could have gotten around intensifying the feelings more than they already were and dealt with it another way. Though, I feel it wouldn't have worked anyway. It's a lost cause.

I am envious of my friend, Mo. He's making it the world so far and has a girl that he's crazy about: my sister. What do I have? Nothing. No sense of belonging anywhere. No girl. And I'm the one who's worked so fucking hard in all my years of therapy exploring a broad range of issues. I am really fucked right now because I go into these rages of anger about how unfair life is. How is talking about it with Dr. M. really going to help me come to terms with it? It's not fair. It's always going to upset me. Why not just think about my struggles when I do and leave it at that? I don't need to be encouraged to discuss it afterward. Anyway, I don't need him. He's full of shit. He wants to take credit for improvements in my life. He tells me that the marijuana was medicating my depression. Well, why couldn't he do that? Why did it get worse and worse? This is with 300mg of Zoloft as well as talking and bringing emotions to the surface. I should not have had moments of relief two years into therapy after which I collapsed into severe suicidal thinking and behavior. But I do feel he understands my case very well and where I've come from. I could, though, explain it to another therapist and I can always come back to Dr.M. if I wanted to.

May 31, 2005

Mo came over and I gave him a birthday gift. He spoke about how he got rewarded for saving a cops life. I can't take it that he's made a life for himself and I can't. When someone close to you has something you don't have it hurts more than someone you're not close to, I guess.

July 3, 2005

I am frustrated and angry that I can't go about getting a girl. When I went outside, I heard Arabic music and I wanted the guy whose radio it came from to start a fight with me. So I looked at him. I can't stand these spiritual thoughts I have regarding the female guest of my mother. My thoughts are that she has come to this community because she has been driven by a higher power so she could meet me. The reasoning behind these thoughts is that because I took the steps to talk to a different girl the other day, a girl will be made available to me. A girl that is more compatible and who will appreciate my qualities.

September 1, 2005

I don't feel so afraid of death because my father said that in Israel when he fell unconscious from dehydration, he felt that it was the best thing to not be here and where there are no worries. I'm worrying about the flood and its destruction in New Orleans. It can happen here and I couldn't take the physical suffering of starving to death.

"Where there is no will, there's no way."

November 24, 2005

Maybe we really don't adapt well to this world where we have to deal with our emotions and all this shit happening to us. We're born with the madness or we're driven to lose our minds. I was a genetic fuck up or bad seed. There is no place for me in this world. Where there is no will, there's no way. I don't have enough of a will to make some other kind of life for myself. I'm stuck in anger and disgusted in life.

February 11, 2006

I haven't written in my diary for a long time because I haven't felt the need to. I've been feeling pretty good. I don't really have anything to feel happy about. I just feel the euphoria. One thing that does help me feel happy is doing crunches on my exercise ball. I started getting deep sleep ever since my grandmother died. I feel really detached. I didn't cry at her funeral but in some way it triggered the nightmares. My neck is hurting now because of the nightmares. It's because of Jake that I feel happy some days but I don't really feel that it's me. Prior to the sessions with Jake, I was emotionally flatlined. I have failed the GED test. I don't have the motivation to study for the next time I take it with extended time.

February 13, 2006

I need an end to this Bullshit. I'm beyond help because I'm beyond the scientific realm of help. I've been helped in a way that no one understands. Everything is more complicated. Physically, I'm weaker. My sinuses seem to be more sensitive to the cold and I get sinus irritation. The physical issues that I already had before I saw Jake became amplified after having seen him. It was a trade-off. As was the weed. It helped at the time but damaged my brain later on. This world is fucked. I don't know what to do. I don't know if Jake's healing will end up lasting and whether the trade-off that occurred will return to its original place or remain. The pain in my ankles are much more difficult to control since I've been doing better mentally. I'm suffering greatly in my mind worrying about that I want to die. Though, I don't want to lose all my belongings. I enjoy my clothing.

February 27, 2006

I was going to Dr.M. planning to stop the therapy cold, as my new therapist said I should, but I agreed to see him three more times. I told Dr. M. I think it would be for the best if the world would come to an end.

March 1, 2006

Today I'm feeling good. I didn't have headaches. I wasn't too nervous. I can't focus on how fucked up the world is. Instead, I'm thinking about how there might be a plan for some people from a higher power. My oldest sister got engaged last night and I feel like maybe this world is not such a bad place after all.

March 12, 2006

My friend wanted me to go out with him to a bar because his girlfriend had a friend that he thought I should meet. I went out and I hurt my left ankle that night. My ankle felt okay in the morning but got worse throughout the day. The pain today is so great that I started myself on antibiotics. It seemed to help a little but when I went to my primary doctor, I had to do some walking and my ankle hurt just as bad. Tonight, my left ankle is killing me. The pain is outrageous. I want an end to this shitty life. It's full of disappointment. Like it says in the Kabbalah book I'm reading: "Man was cursed from the time Adam ate the forbidden fruit". The whole thing is Bullshit. Who's to judge how much choice he had. Not even the creator has a right to judge because he is unjust.

April 5, 2006

I listened to my recorded session with Dr.M. from the time after I started smoking marijuana. This was before I lost my mind from the withdrawal. I recorded him without his knowledge. He told me that it's like we were not working together when I told him I was recording. Damn straight. I was self-medicating using the marijuana because he couldn't help me. He was too slow to realize his failures as a therapist. It makes me think how in life people do the best they can to solve problems. And, if they fail lives could be at stake. From looking back at my life, it really seems there was no path for me and there still isn't. I am probably more into the gloomy picture of life at the present moment because my throat hurts. Although the pessimistic outlook is real, that doesn't mean I can't be pessimistic and enjoy whatever I can, simultaneously. This only happens when Jake and the meds are holding me.

April 7, 2006

I'm feeling so nervous walking to Duane Reade. I was ready to take Clonazepam but I decided that I wasn't going to fight the nervousness but accept the fact that people notice me being nervous. I started not feeling as nervous after that. I am so unstable emotionally. I had bad nightmares last night. I awoke screaming. Someone was trying to steal my bike from me. The dream about the bike wasn't terrifying until the very end of my dream when I woke up. I was mostly dreaming of traveling around the neighborhood.

April 21, 2006

I am very disgusted with life. I can't help but think about the Holocaust and how the Jews were slaughtered like sheep. Then, leaders of the community push the Jews to multiply while we are in dark times. Who knows what's next?

Perhaps six billion Jews dying over a nuclear attack. I know that this negative or pessimistic thinking isn't good for my nightmares but I can't help it.

April 22, 2006

I didn't want to eat with the family tonight because I knew that I would just bring the family down and into my darkness. I did eat with them in the end. I kept silent most of the time. I feel very distant from my father. I'm angry with him because he doubts the whole religion and when I do something that's wrong on the Sabbath he gets upset. For example, I picked up the soup from the flame after having removed the lid, which is prohibited on the Shabbat. He became really angry at me for doing that because now my family can't use the pot for the rest of the Shabbat. He's full of shit just like everyone else in this world. We are such conflicted beings. Our experiences in life bring about conflicted views in us at different times. When things are going better for me, I take in the possibility that there is a plan or heavenly intervention. Right now I'm so sure there isn't anything of the sort. I just think life is meaningless. I want to get it over with it as soon as possible. As depressed as I feel, I still take care of myself. I brushed and flossed my teeth. I was contemplating not doing it.

May 6, 2006

I just finished seeing the movie called, "The Island", and one thought I had was that with the miracles of modern science, there are going to be way too many people in the world with more old people than ever before and more births. So many things are off in the world, putting my life aside, which is and was fucked to the worst degree. I do know one thing and that is, since I've seen Jake, my body doesn't heal itself the way it used to and I come down with viruses and bacterial infections more often now than before.

May 7, 2006

I think the human condition sucks so much. I'm so disturbed by what I've been through. The whole human race is so unbalanced. There are way too many things that could go wrong. We are such complex beings. It just shouldn't be. After watching a documentary on the Holocaust, I'm really not expecting anything to come of my life. Any heavenly intervention is highly unlikely to happen. To see people murdered like that shows that humans mean nothing to the creator and they serve no profound purpose. This is some kind of sick game being played on us. Many humans do come out normal. In fact, probably most do. I guess just a small portion of unfortunate people, like myself, have to suffer to no end until our body's finally fail us. But then something big happens, let's say a nuclear attack, everyone's affected and the whole human race is fucked. Am I just focusing on the negative causing the world to seem darker than it is? Or is it really hopeless? It's a combination. I'm focusing more on the negative and maybe ignoring the positive but the outcome is the same. There is no solution to the human problem. It can't be fixed.

May 13, 2006

I was feeling upset and depressed from the drinking of a mixed liquor concoction that my older brother made last night. Today I feel very gloomy and depressed. I was feeling a little better later in the day. I watched, "The Butterfly Effect", and it makes me think that I really have to be careful which college I go to and what girls I get involved with. There doesn't seem to be a plan for me in this life. I don't care to live. In the movie, I realized what being real is. In one of the scenes, the actor is acting himself but his girlfriend isn't. I am a real person not just putting on an act, but acting on my own wiring of my brain, not others'. My brain has a lot of faulty wiring. The fact is that I can't deal with girls or guys in these colleges. There are so few people like me. People seem to just want to have a good time without being themselves. To deal with their inner demons is painful, so why do it? Don't be yourself, be someone else. My own actions and personality were shaped a lot by the therapy I was in, the marijuana smoking as well as the healing done by Jake. How much more real am I than those fakes out there? There's no difference, except, I'm different than most of the world. It really sucks to be me. To be lonely forever. I'm different than the majority in so many ways. Wake up to reality. There is no reality.

May 16, 2006

I was watching the news channel. They were discussing that America is the greatest country to go to. They were discussing this issue with illegal immigration. I started to think that my life is not so bad. I'm in the greatest country in the world.

It's as though it takes away from the outrageous suffering I've gone through mentally all these years. It may be the greatest country in the world but we may not have the greatest minds in this country compared to the rest of the world. In America, we don't suffer as much physically, in terms of having food to eat, but mentally, boy do we suffer!

May 18, 2006

I went to group therapy and I got into a heated debate about free will. It was really me versus the whole group. No one else thinks like me and I want them to. I became tense so I wasn't as clear as I wanted to be. The therapist said that I wasn't thinking it through and that my view is flawed. He was proving that people do have free-will. He used this scenario to prove his point: If there was a police man with an abuser with his victim in the same room, the abuser wouldn't attack his victim. I didn't have a response. Later, I was thinking how flawed his argument was. In the above scenario, it doesn't mean the abuser has control over his actions. Maybe in this instance it would be considered he didn't even have a choice to do it because of retribution from the policemen. He didn't have a choice or, really, an equal choice. The pull in this scenario to not engage in his abusive behavior may be stronger than to engage. I'm not saying that the abuser should get away with his actions. He should know that there are consequences for his actions. There won't always be a motive to not engage in his abusive behavior because consequences may not be right in front of the person.

In normal circumstances, the pull to engage in such behavior could be stronger. But it isn't fair that the person is held responsible because if he lacks control, he can't help himself but do it. But life is not fair. For instance, the situation with me bothering my little sister. After the heated debate, I was feeling really upset when I met my parents at CVS pharmacy to take me out for my birthday

May 20, 2006

I am so sexually frustrated I can't take it anymore. I'm so disturbed by my dreams. I get into this mood where nothing matters to me and I want to put a stop to this hell. I guess I should find a way that I am capable to end this life. I like the risky behavior that I start to have when I'm in a suicidal mode. If I succeed in killing myself, at least I'll have succeeded in something in this life. I welcome my pessimistic views and suicidality when I'm sexually frustrated because it helps take the edge off of it.

May 21, 2006

I'm thinking: Why not just go to a bunch of psychic healers for the hell of it? I was feeling very suicidal the past few days. Why should I care if I get screwed in the process? My mind was not clear either for the past few days and I'm also suffering greatly mentally. It hurts me so much that I can't play the drums. I was so good at it. I worked so hard on them and then they were taken from me.

June 6, 2006

I went to my psychiatrist walking as though I didn't care about anything. Nothing scared me, not even girls. I was just pissed off. My psychiatrist decided to try a new medicine called Elavil to help alleviate my anxiety and depression. I called Jake to ask him if I should try this new medicine. He said it feels right for me to start.

June 10, 2006

I think I'm going to stop taking the Elavil. I slept all day today and last night I was feeling very tired. I was feeling nervous when I woke up so I took Clonazepam and that knocked me out. Tonight, I feel nervous and I'm back in the depressed mode. I am feeling a little nauseous and weak. I don't care to live life. This medication sucks.

June 11, 2006

I stopped taking Elavil today. I feel horrible. I'm emotionally so down, I can't smile. I spoke to my mother very angrily about how this game of life is disgusting and that I'm being played and abused in it. This so-called setup of life is far from perfect. I feel bad that I spoke to her like that. She can't deal with that gloominess. It hurts her too much to hear me talk like that. This talk is exactly what she didn't want to hear from my father when that's what he talked about. Now her suffering is multiplied by me and other kids in the family who share mental agony and see the true reality of life, which seems to not be very good.

June 13, 2006

I'm in a much lighter mood the past two days. Maybe the Saint John's wort is helping.

June 15, 2006

I'm not doing well. Yesterday, all I thought about was how much I want to kill myself because I know that my emotional health won't hold. I may be thinking more clearly but the mental pain is outrageous. I was very agitated today so I took clonazepam. After I went to group therapy, I was feeling a little better with my mood but I just fell back into agitation. I'm in prison in my head. All I want is to be released. I know that means death but I welcome it to the fullest. I don't want the suffering before I die but as they say the juice (death) is worth the squeeze, i.e., to squeeze this godforsaken life out of me. This life sickens me. I'm feeling very sexually frustrated tonight. What the hell am I supposed to do with myself? I'm so freaking scared of girls. The question is not where did things go wrong with me, it's when were things ever right? Everything in nature is out of whack. It's imbalanced. It's wrong for humans to exist under these conditions.

June 16, 2006

I'm feeling a lot better emotionally. I feel a little agitated at times. I'm afraid that I'm going to get sucked back into the hell. I'm happy that I almost completed learning the Chopin song by heart.

June 17, 2006

The nightmares last night were outrageous. I was going through a replay of being in a situation where I was with a bunch of high school classmates. In my dream I was older and was visiting the school. I was acting a certain way and I couldn't figure out why. Whatever I was doing caused a commotion with other kids. Then the principal yelled at me in front of thousands of kids telling me look at what I've done. I can't live with these night terrors. Finally, after dreaming the same scenario over and over, I wake up. The dreams were terrifying as hell. It makes me contemplate suicide. Then, I was thinking about my little sister and how she has avoided going through what I went through— that I had to be the one to go through hell. Maybe if I would kill myself it would have a major impact on her and then she would have to deal with pain like what I went through. My brain feels so imbalanced. I do not want anyone to go through what I go through. As the day went on, I got into a more positive mood despite those horrific dreams. I'm upset that I had them. I had bad headaches today.

June 20, 2006

I'm feeling okay emotionally today, though, I don't care to live. I also went through times of being sucked into feeling agitated. I don't care that I may be damaging my skin in the sun. I don't care for my body to last long anyway. At least I'll look good for now. I'm anyway not going to look good at thirty or at least my looks will be going downhill by then. It's shocking that I'll be thirty in five years. That's crazy. I shouldn't have gotten this far in life considering that I abused substances to rid my suffering.

June 24, 2006

Today was a terrible day. I had nightmares last night. I'm so agitated right now and I want to kill myself somehow. I hate life. I've collapsed emotionally. I want to die already. This life is so meaningless. My suffering is pointless. The human condition sucks. We shouldn't even exist. There's no one in control of our existence. It finally seems that if people want to have kids, they can prevent birth defects and choose if it should be male or female. So who's in control now? It sure seems we are. We have to run this world because there is no heavenly intervention because life stinks. It's fucked up. I don't want to exist anymore. Just put me out of my misery. Let me just not wake up tomorrow morning. I'd love to die in my sleep.

June 26, 2006

I've come down with either a virus or bacterial infection. My throat hurts and I feel weak. I am feeling horrible emotionally. I'm so upset and agitated. I just want to die. This life is messed up. My whole life there has been battles going on in my body with other forms of life which made me sick. Well, not life, the living organisms trying to take over my body. My body will battle and try to rid the bad and try to repair itself as part of its program. One species feeding off of another. It's completely meaningless. I go through way too much suffering. Let this virus take over me and die together with me because it can't survive unless I'm alive. Once I'm dead it has won the battle. It will have taken me over.

June 28, 2006

I'm feeling more upbeat today. I was talking with people in the family, acting humorous and also speaking about how it's not fair for people to go to such extremes with emotional suffering. For instance, my oldest sister is under a lot of pressure. She doesn't know whether or not she should get married.

June 29, 2006

I was feeling alright emotionally earlier today, regardless of feeling sicker from this infection in my throat and sinuses. I started taking Omnicef and that causes me to feel like shit emotionally. I'm so agitated now, I can't speak to anyone. Before I took the antibiotics, I was acting silly and was able to talk to people. Now I want to end this life.

July 4, 2006

I'm feeling good emotionally but my sinuses are still a problem. It's a little better today. I'm not depressed today but I still keep in mind that this world is fucked and I talk about it. However, I don't get sucked into a gloomy mood where it affects my ability to enjoy moments of life.

July 7, 2006

I had to take clonazepam at my oldest sister's wedding and I hadn't slept much the night before. I was very sleepy during the wedding and didn't enjoy it. It was a pain in the ass. Today I'm feeling very agitated and I felt so crippled by my anxiety. It was torture to walk outside. I took clonazepam and after half an hour to 45 minutes I started feeling relaxed. I didn't care what people thought of me. I went to physical therapy today and from there I went to BMCC. All of a sudden, my stomach started to hurt and I had to take a shit. I lost control and shit came out as I was crossing the street. I then went into a restaurant, sat on their toilet seat and had to wipe myself up which took forever. I hate life. I think that I am back to the spiritual thinking of the possibility that there is a plan and path for me in this world. I still think that this existence is an accident and a very bad one at that. I can't stand switching back and forth on these views. Besides, I'm not thinking clearly these days. Maybe it's because of the antibiotics. The one big thing that makes me want to go on with life is the desire to experience something with females.

July 8, 2006

I didn't take yesterday's dose of antibiotics because I can't stand that it causes me to have an upset stomach. I only took Omnicef for seven days. I feel so angry after watching the movie, *Flight 93*, last night. I drank vodka, got a little twisted and acted crazy. Last night I had terrible nightmares. I must have forgotten to take one of my medications. I don't care anymore.

Why should I bother fighting this infection? Just let it take over me, win the battle and end my stupid life because I don't care. The only thing I can get out of life now is girls but I can give that up for death. I hate life. I really feel weak and nauseous now. Fuck it!

July 10, 2006

I went to BMCC in the morning. I was so nervous that I had to take clonazepam for the orientation at 10 AM. Then I took the placement tests for college. I failed the math completely. I don't want to learn that shit. I'm only going to college because I have nothing better to do with my time. I have to remind myself that when I start taking college too seriously, I'm not doing it to pass. Though, I might have to pass in order for the state to pay for my college tuition. But if I don't get good enough grades, I'll have to pay out of pocket. I had headaches right before I took the test. I took Advil and that helped. Both of my wrists hurt right now. I played the piano for too long and that's why my wrists hurt. I feel a little good about having finished learning the complete song of Chopin on the piano.

July 17, 2006

Today was my first day at the BMCC. I don't like it because when I try to think of problems to solve, for example math, my head starts hurting. My head was hurting even before I went to school but trying to concentrate makes it worse. I'm feeling very nervous today in general. I also want an end to my life. I'm sick of being alive, I'm sick of being human.

July 19, 2006

I can't take this fucking life anymore. I can't take this school shit. I don't want to learn math. I'm not going to meet people like myself in college. There is no one like me. I am fucked up. I just want to die already. I can't make a life for myself. All I think about is suicide. I want out of this world. I don't want to do things that are difficult which is everyday survival. I don't want to learn math in order to go to classes I'm interested in. Basically, I can't make a life for myself in this way. I need to be in a relaxing setting and occupy my time in a simple way, maybe being a janitor or garbage collector. I would so much rather not deal with life. Today in college, I was having such a nervous feeling and was panicking, so I took clonazepam. I am feeling the way I would feel whenever I would go take a new job.

July 22, 2006

I'm doing terrible lately. I'm having nightmares at night and during the day when I take a nap. My thoughts about life are fucked up. I think about how we are just like other species with just a greater awareness of the things around us. That humans run on instinct. I canceled the summer classes in college because my anxiety was way too high.

July 29, 2006

I am having terrible nightmares lately and bad headaches during the day. Last night I had horrific nightmares, reliving my experience when I got overwhelmed two weeks ago in college. I slept all day today and had a much deeper sleep and now I feel very agitated. I don't have clarity in my thinking.

August 1, 2006

Girls are so different than guys. Girls like drama and poetry. Guys like sex. The only thing in common with both sexes is their desire in the physical counterparts. But, because we can speak and have emotions, it fucks up the whole process of ever getting a girl. I have to forget about getting one. I hope that I won't live long. I can't suffer with this frustration anymore and I most definitely can't approach a woman. I was feeling nervous tonight just speaking to my younger brother. There are lots of people fucked up in this world. This is a world that should not be. This place is insane. Everything is backwards. Too many things are wrong. If the cells in the human body can't follow the instructions properly then I suppose we shouldn't be. There's way too much suffering when things do go wrong with people.

August 7, 2006

I'm not thinking sharp lately. It's not terrible but it's not so good. I went to BMCC to register for classes. I don't know if I can make it. I think I'll go way up on the Zoloft so that maybe I'll have a chance of not getting so overwhelmed. I was so overwhelmed during summer classes that I wasn't planning on registering for college but only to sit in the classes. I had a bad headache today after dealing with college. I had nightmares about being in a school setting and getting overwhelmed that I had to leave the program. When I sit in the sun for a long time it seems to trigger my nightmares.

August 8, 2006

I went up on the Zoloft to 250 mg in hope that when I go to college I'll be less overwhelmed. I'm feeling very agitated when going to my primary care physician. I'm feeling horrible today and very nervous that I couldn't sleep last night or during the day. My ankle is hurting a lot today. I was going to use a cane to help me walk to my doctor but the thought of it was making me really nervous. I'm afraid of walking down the street and losing control with the anxiety of people looking at me.

August 17, 2006

I'm having so much rage against religion. I can't see people following the rules. I can't say the words from the siddur. It just disgusts me. I had dreams of rage last night of a heated argument with my oldest brother about whether we are fit to be on this planet. I said that because of our emotions we're not fit. When something happens that we can't handle, we lose our emotional balance or at least the balance that we consider normal (because the majority of people are a certain way). All I know is that I don't think I'll get a girl because I can't play the role that would make the females like me. A role that is not controlled by their beauty and the whole cat and mouse game.

Females play hard to get, which is a trait of all species of birds or animals. I'm so disturbed right now that I want to see life on earth destroyed. I don't feel it's fair to have such a defective world and the people that are defective are blamed and punished for what they do. It makes us all guilty in a sense because we don't make who we are. It's genetics and environment both of which fucked me up. I am so disgusted when I see guys staring at girls' asses. I feel it's so ridiculous to focus attraction to that area of the female body. My experience in life is ruined so it would be fine if was over.

August 21, 2006

I'm having one nightmare after the next. I feel sleepy during the day. Dr. S. said I should go way up on the Trileptal. He wants me to go up 75 mg, seven times the amount I want to. I'll try it. I am very agitated today and all I want is to die. I have an appointment with Rob, who is a chiropractor/healer, tomorrow. I don't even care if he messes things up with my head because I feel the end of the world is near. It's such a comforting thought sometimes but now it's disturbing me.

August 23, 2006

This chiropractor is not a healer like Jake and I don't think he could help me. My body has gotten slower to heal, thanks to Jake. My body also gets injured easier and I'm more sensitive to pain. I don't think he can make much of a difference.

August 28, 2006

I was feeling very disturbed while watching a documentary about a spy that was in the US. It was about Mohammed Sheikh Ali who was working for Al Qaeda and the US. Al Qaeda really wants to destroy us because of our troops being in their land, which according to the US, is for humane reasons. It was because of the way they treat their citizens, where the government takes all the money and doesn't give it to their people. Our government wants to change that. Now we are in a big mess because they are determined to destroy us. We can't reason with them because the extremists want to take over the whole world like the Nazi's tried.

August 29, 2006

I saw Jake today. I feel emotionally unstable as is expected when I see him. Then, in time, I tend to bounce back emotionally. I'm feeling down emotionally since I watched a documentary about a spy in the US. It's so depressing. Seeing bodies being carried like dolls in the concentration camps after they were killed by starvation was also disturbing. I start school tomorrow. I'm not feeling scared but I know that I get overwhelmed when there's girls around and I get distracted from the teacher if they're sitting next to me.

September 6, 2006

I had bad nightmares last night again. The first part of the nightmare was vivid but not painful. Except, one of the parts of the dream there was a car explosion and I was in the path of the explosion feeling the heat pass over me. I wasn't frightened. After, I had very painful dreams about rage being directed at me for not controlling my behavior with my youngest sister. She ripped a button from my jacket. When I woke up I was thinking whether it's worth it to go through all this pain to go to college. I can't raise the dosage of the Trileptal until I'm on my settled dose of Cymbalta. Maybe it's the wrong time to try a new medicine. Maybe I should just go up on the Trileptal and stop taking the Cymbalta for now. As stress escalates, so do my nightmares and they are harder to control with the use of drugs. My brain is so fucked. When I wake up from the dreams, I'm put in a very disturbed mood and have suicidal thoughts. I'm feeling sleepy now even though I took a two hour nap. I probably will have nightmares again tonight which is what usually happens when I feel sleepy the way I do now.

September 10, 2006

I was watching a TV segment about the Holocaust and I was thinking, "What makes me so special that things in my life should turn out for the better while 6 million Jews waited for their death?"

September 12, 2006

I'm in a better mood today but I had a headache later in the day, probably related to stress from college. It's so hard for me to believe and except that I'm in college. I don't like when my parents express their happiness that I'm attending college. I used the Imitrex nasal spray. It seemed to help with the tension headache for a while but now it's back. I feel nervous about the test coming up and I can't control the excitement. I'm not really worried about failing but I'm worrying anyway because I want to do well. I want to feel accomplished with something in my life. I am concerned that when it comes to the test, I will not know a lot of the information and won't pass.

September 17, 2006

I had very deep sleep last night. When I woke up I wasn't sure what day it was. Dr.M. was in my dream. I refused to get involved in a scary real-life déjà vu' scenario, but at the same time, it seemed like a movie that I was in—involved yet detached. I decided not to watch it because I had remembered it scared the shit out of me in the past. I felt I could fall into the terror. Dr. M. was telling people in the so-called movie that they are envious.

September 20, 2006

I tried to kill a big bug in my room last night but it was too hard to kill because it was huge. I tried to capture it but it ran too fast. When I squashed it I hurt it, but it got away. I found it in my room today so I captured it and brought it outside. I was feeling horrible that I didn't kill it and now it's suffering like I am. I'm not feeling good today. I'm feeling nervous and depressed. I was speaking to this guy that's going to psychology class with me and he wanted to take the quiz with me. I feel so uncomfortable around him because I'm not on the same page communication wise. I also feel like I'm lowering my status by hanging around him.

September 23, 2006

This world sucks. I hope the news that my father told me about Bin Laden planning a nuclear attack on all major cities in the US is accurate. I've been feeling like shit for the past few days. I'm extremely nervous and I don't feel comfortable around people. I wasn't sure how I feel about life and whether I want to die or not. Now I am sure. My life is so fucked. There was no reason to keep me in this world while I was suffering so much. It's been like that since high school. Let this world go back to stardust and never be allowed to form life as we know it. That's one wish I have now. Nothing can be made right with my life now that Jake changed my whole brain. I wish somehow I was able to kill myself because if not, I'll have to suffer double with a nuke attack. All this suffering in my life was for nothing. Life isn't meaningful. There's no point to this shit. I don't see the whole picture but life is not right. The process of destruction shall begin now.

September 25, 2006

I am doing terrible again today. I'm so depressed that I'm having thoughts about death. I was feeling so depressed in school today that I didn't smile at anyone. I was so angry. I took Clonazepam and that took the edge off of the depression. I was getting headaches all day. I couldn't get rid of the headache tonight. I don't know how I'm feeling right now. I'm trying to learn psychology even with all this shit going on because I want to do well on my exam. I also want to know the information for myself. I spoke to the teacher after class trying to understand what she was talking about. Nobody would ever know what I'm going through.

October 17, 2006

I've been having days of depression. Yesterday I was feeling very depressed. Today I'm not feeling depressed as much. I don't know if my thoughts on life are distorted or if life is really fucked up. I know my life is, but I feel that there shouldn't be human life at all. I don't think the combination of our desires or fantasies and our reflections on them mix well when it comes to being able to have sex. Sex is all about reproducing. Even the marijuana plant has a male and female part and it does what's natural. Everything on this planet is here for the sake of reproduction but why reproduce the human species? I think the human species should be extinct. Just leave it to the insects and other mammals. I can't communicate with my parents. In fact, I wish I didn't have to see them because all they do is annoy me. They brought me down right when I happened to be in a good mood. It's a shame that I can't have a relationship with my parents. I'm upset with the lot I've been dealt. I'm an alien.

October 24, 2006

I've been having headaches the past week. It's a little less than it was last week; I don't feel a headache all the time. I can't study with a headache. I'm not sure if it's a tension headache or sinusitis. Either way, stress or excitement brings it on. I need a girl badly. I will take this antipsychotic and hope it will eliminate my need for girls. I want to want a girl, but the frustration is too great that I'd rather get rid of it for now. I'm not ready for it anyway.

October 25, 2006

I took Geodon last night and I was feeling very drowsy this morning. I felt dizzy and couldn't walk straight. I didn't go to college today because of it. I'm having headaches today. I won't be taking Geodon anymore. My mood is a lot more positive after I read my diary. I think Cymbalta is kicking in. I also haven't been having nightmares. I don't know if that's related to the Cymbalta, but since my nightmares have let down, I've been having tension headaches almost constantly.

October 30, 2006

I had nightmares last night. I was in a physical fight with my high school principal. Today was my psychology test. I took Clonazepam and Maxalt and I didn't have to deal with a headache. I'm in a better mood than I have been in the past week. I'm having headaches on and off. I'm obsessional about my disgust with sexuality. I don't feel in need of a girl today. Instead, I just feel disgusted with having physical contact with the opposite sex. I understand that attraction is mostly just nature's way of getting us to reproduce. I know humans are able to defeat the whole reason we have sex with intellect. We can now have sex for the sake of pleasure without it resulting in having kids. Nevertheless, this whole process disgusts me. Maybe this is just pure insanity on my part based on a really shitty life experience and due to the use of drugs.

November 6, 2006

I'm feeling terrible emotionally. I'm going through an episode of a severe suicidal state and depression. I really want an end to this life. It's not worth it to go through all this bullshit just to get bits of pleasure from life, which in itself is rare. I keep having disturbed thoughts of disgust towards sex. The production of a child gets me thinking of the parents that produced them. This grosses me out. I feel this is the worst form of life and should be ended.

November 8, 2006

I finally got a break from this episode I've been going through. I'm feeling less depressed. I'm not enraged by everything and less agitated.

November 15, 2006

The past few days I've been on an emotional rollercoaster. During the day my mood changes from being happy to being very upset accompanied with disturbing thoughts. Today my disturbed thoughts were about sex and how disgusted I am that I have this strong driving urge to be with a woman. This is all part of this setup of life that I'm very much against—having sex to reproduce. This driving urge is just to get us to continue this species. I don't see why life should be since we are faced with impossible situations at times. For instance, I was seeing Dr. M. and getting involved with smoking weed. When the only option available is to take a path of destruction, it means that I'm not for this life. Even though there's a minority of people faced with this, I am part of this minority. At least I have not been having many headaches. I filled out my transfer application for Kingsborough. Hopefully, in the spring when I go to classes, I'll be around plenty of women.

Part Three

Paradox

November 17, 2006

It really sucks. It seems that the only way to get a girl to be attracted to you is to not be yourself. If you're a nice guy you'll be put in the friend zone. Girls get turned off when you're nice to them, yet they say they want a nice, sensitive guy. They don't know what they want. They think they want a nice guy but it's a jerk that really turns them on. The girls that you don't show interest in are going to want you because they want what they feel they can't have. You really have to be a player to get with a girl. A nice guy can't be his real self—he'll kill the attraction. You have to banter with a woman; tease her, control her and tell her what to do. Otherwise, you don't seem in control. A girl wants a man that is in control of himself and not controlled by the woman's beauty. It seems that girls have it so easy. They can just act like themselves and get the man they desire in a heartbeat. But men have to manipulate women. Humans are such conflicted beings.

"Whatever force is behind nature, I would not put my trust in it and have kids."

November 21, 2006

I would be a great kind of guy for a long term relationship—nice, sensitive and caring. All which would have to be without my psychological problems. Here I am having qualities for a long-term relationship which I don't want, but I don't have qualities for a short-term one which is basically being a jerk. I won't be able to get what I want from a girl unless I find one that is disabled like me and doesn't want anything serious. Chances are very slim. People keep things to themselves. I've been preoccupied with the thought that the world should not have gone past World War II and by stopping World War II, we have pushed off the inevitable of a world war III. So, unnecessary suffering has been the result. Life doesn't have to go on. I feel manipulated by nature, in a sense, with having sexual urges and its way of getting us to reproduce. We are hijacked to fulfill natures cause. Whatever force is behind nature, I would not put my trust in it and have kids. Nature is too god damned screwed up with humans hating each other and all.

November 26, 2006

It moved me after my father helped me buy a bass guitar, I hugged him. That brought him to tears and he said he loves me. This made me cry after having gone to my room. I was thinking about all the suffering I've had to endure. My nightmares have been very intense lately. Last night, I dreamt I was at a meeting with a dating coach, David DeAngelo and this kid took my seat. There was fighting with lots of rage. I woke up sweating a lot.

November 27, 2006

I'm feeling a little better today. I was feeling very upset while in school. I'm just hoping for an end to this life. I took the psychology exam. I think I did well but I don't really care that much. A thought that goes through my mind is that since I may be smart, I should hang on a little longer to see were life can take me. Life has outrageous suffering and I don't have peace of mind.

November 29, 2006

I'm feeling very shitty today. I was feeling so miserable and I got into my suicidal thinking. I was thinking about how badly I want to have a gun and shoot my brains out. I like to imagine the pain while I'm dying and thinking that I've finally succeeded in killing myself. Dr. Lee, the behaviorist, thinks that I can learn to control my thoughts. He thinks I can restructure my thoughts so I have a choice to not have disturbing thoughts. It might be that I can learn to do that but what about the mental pain I experience. I know my thoughts can contribute to my suffering but sometimes it's my mental pain contributing to my negative thoughts and to think at this point I can control them is unrealistic. What I have is a physical defect. There's brain damage from smoking pot and from my nervous breakdown in high school. Dr. Lee thinks by restructuring your thoughts, you can fix physical parts of your brain.

December 7, 2006

I'm not doing well emotionally today. I feel like things are going down a path to doom. I believe that there is no path for me in this world. I don't believe there is a kind God that intends good things for us humans. I believe he doesn't care much at all. All I want is to be gone from this hell. I feel my brain has been destroyed with the use of drugs. My views are probably distorted because of it but I believe these things right now. I think America is in a big mess with Iraq and I think the world will face a scenario similar to my own where it's damned if you do and damned if you don't. Basically, we're fucked. Throughout history, a person would rise and predict the coming of the Messiah and it didn't come. What makes our times different than then? What we can hope for is the end to human suffering by an end to all life on earth through a nuclear disaster. This will be fine.

December 18, 2006

I've been feeling terrible the past few days. My anxiety was so high yesterday that I wanted to end my life. My views are so far from what others think. I don't think I should be around anymore. The thought that stopped me from doing anything to harm myself, was the thought that if I don't end my suffering, I'll be around when a natural disaster or terrorism happens. I'm like a pest, a nuisance to my little sister. I can't control my abuse towards her. I'm suffering way too much and have had enough. Next time I come down with a bacterial infection, I won't take care of it and it will hopefully end my life. I can't have anything I want or need in life and I can't stick around and bear the pain. Maybe I have some qualities to offer others but it's just not worth the pain. Last night I was feeling so angry and suicidal I couldn't study for the psychology exam. I then took clonazepam and felt more relaxed. Last night was my worst case of anxiety in a long time. The pain in my mind was outrageous. I had bad nightmares and woke up feeling very strange.

My spiritual thoughts about there being a spirit out there with a plan came back because I passed the writing exam which I spent almost four hours taking. But, when I was sitting at my desk contemplating suicide, I was thinking I could just end it right now. What kind of path could that be? I may be especially anxious since it's the end of the semester and I would like to attend Kingsborough next semester. New situations throw me off emotionally.

December 23, 2006

I started taking Requip and I had to stop it on Friday night because I've been feeling flu-like symptoms. I've been feeling nauseous and weak. I've been waking up at 5 AM for the past two nights while I was taking it. I wouldn't be able to keep up with the cocky funny attitude that coincides with David DeAngelo's theory on women and dating. This is all to make a woman feel more comfortable. Though, if I don't feel comfortable and I lose my cool, I will look like a wimp to a woman. I'm not a real man.

December 26, 2006

I saw my psychiatrist today. She says my brain really is screwed up. My brain doesn't respond to the medication the way normal people's brains do. I don't want this life if my thoughts which reflect my feelings are caused by chemical changes in the brain. Nothing is real this way. When I feel optimistic about life it's not reality-based but at least it feels good. When I'm pessimistic, it is very much reality-based because I got screwed over and over again in my life. I don't think I can fix these problems that I have. It's way over my head to deal with them. I can only hope that somehow I will be killed in some disaster. I have to re-experience the pain of losing my ability to play the drums every time I play them. I can't get back into drumming and I may not be able to get into playing the bass because that also irritates my wrists. My love for music is really for the drums and I've lost them. The human body doesn't seem to be designed for repetitive movement. Why do we humans have a need to play music? I don't know if the human body was designed for the survival of our species. How are human emotions for the sake of continuing the human species when our emotions get in the way of doing just that—having sex? A male wants to have sex but the female has all these feelings of being used for just sex. She wants to be appreciated for the person she is, not just for her physical appearance. Aids will probably kill a large number of humans. One could ask, 'How is nature setting the stage for the survival of certain species if the species has other life forms to just destroy it?' I'm just sick of this whole life process. I don't enjoy it at all. What the hell is this place? Whatever it is, it sets the stage for hell on earth.

December 30, 2006

I went last night to a bar to see a friend play the drums. I drank two beers after taking Clonazepam to help relax me but it just made my mind feel blank. My plan was to try to get a girl's phone number and e-mail address but I got way too nervous. The drinking brought on thoughts of why save someone's life when a person gets hurt. I was thinking this because I went on a call with my friend who's a paramedic where a person got mugged and they rushed him to the hospital. I'm feeling very depressed and suicidal. I had nightmares last night. It was very painful dreams of my sexual frustration. It was so painful. My thoughts of suicide gave me a bad headache, so I took Geodon. I don't feel that if I actually hurt myself that someone should save me. I'm suffering and if I have to end my suffering by killing myself, so be it. If I did kill myself, people would say I'm selfish because I'm causing my family pain by doing it. But what about my pain? They can't take that away from me. It's selfish of them not to let me kill myself.

January 6 2007

My nightmares were unbelievable last night. It was just going on all night and the dreams were very vivid. I had dreams of rage towards my older brother. I woke up kicking because I was trying to kick him in my dream. We were having a physical fight. Overall I was in a good mood today despite my nightmares. I was feeling very nervous walking to the park today. I played the bass and now my left wrist is hurting. I feel like my wrists are getting weaker and weaker. It took three and a half weeks for my wrists to finally heal from drumming at a friend's house. Tonight, my thoughts have shifted more negatively about life. What's the point of getting involved in the short-term pleasures in life, like playing a musical instrument or having a girlfriend? Of course these are needs and I need them for survival. But why survive? I would be fine with leaving it all behind and end all my conflicts. Then, I brush my teeth and take care of myself. It's all so puzzling to me how I am ready to die and then shift in mood when it's time to care for myself. I sit in my room, surf the web and watch movies. All I have is my thoughts and I feel that my thoughts are way off. I don't feel there's a point in thinking about life. It's all just phases in life that create certain patterns of thinking and it all amounts to nothing because it's all based on theory or experience one has in life.

What's the point of using someone's theory, let's say evolution, and use that as a means to communicate? It's like birds chirping and it's all bullshit. We only communicate because we're social creatures. I don't feel such clarity in my thoughts. My nightmares have cranked up five notches and it's probably due to me planning to attend Kingsborough community college. My therapist told me Friday that life has a way of turning things around. It was as though he was saying that life has some form of balance. It's a pretty terrible balance. Nevertheless, I was thinking I will have my chance and things will become better for me in the future after all the shit I've been through.

January 9, 2007

Last night I had the worst nightmares I've had in a while. I dreamt the doctor was doing a procedure on my heart and he gave me a pill. I experienced my heart stopping and incredible pain that was so vivid and real. I was very upset when I woke up that I went through so much pain in my sleep. My mind is ruined from the drug use. I don't think I'll get my nightmares to go away for good.

January 16, 2007

Where am I in my mind? I'm so not in the same reality as people around me. I'm against procreation. Even though I enjoy my brother's kids, I think there's potential for way too much suffering. I bring it up with my mother over and over again when she gets enthusiastic about children. It especially bothers me when she says she would love to have another child. Which reality is she in? Doesn't she realize her family has gone through enough and having another child would mean more suffering? More pleasure for her perhaps, but it might not be so for that child. I could consider myself to have gone mad but I strongly believe that since in life the pain a person experiences can reach uncharted territory, life shouldn't exist. Earth shouldn't support life as we know it. The whole setup of wanting a girl is bugging me. It's so foreign to me that we desire another human body. It's all for the sake of continuing this species. It does seem that there's some sort of design when I think about it; something designed life so that forms of life should mate with one another in order for that species to continue. If a being within a species is found unattractive to the opposite sex, then those genes will go extinct. If girls like to date only jerks and have sex with them, then the genetics of nice guys will go extinct. Women say they want nice guys but they tend to fall for guys that seem in control of things: A guy that's a jerk. I don't want a life similar to mine to continue in the future. I want my genes to go extinct. Humans probably have similar nervous systems as mice and other species. I wonder if humans are the only species that are so screwed up.

January 28, 2007

Today I went to white planes to celebrate my aunt and uncle's anniversary party. There was this girl that was really cute and I was contemplating saying something to her. I finally had it in me, with a push from my sister, to go over to her. I went over and asked if she has an e-mail address and she said she didn't. Then I asked her if she has electricity and she said yes. I asked for her telephone number and she said she has a boyfriend. I'm not taking this rejection seriously. I think of it as practice.

February 26, 2007

I started college today. I feel like shit. The medication is not working now. I'm thinking about how we evolved from rats and other rodents. I'm so angry with life and everyone. I have no way of getting a girl. I'm too nervous and I don't even feel comfortable just being friendly with them. I'm very agitated today. Everything gets on my fucking nerves.

March 4, 2007

I'm not doing well at all today. I'm going through so much pain in my mind. I had nightmares last night. I'm filled with uncontrollable rage towards my parents for following the religion. But mostly I'm disgusted with life and feel that humans are a by-product of nature gone awry.

March 12, 2007

I feel like I'm coming down with something. I wish my osteomyelitis took me out when I was eight years old. I could have been spared a lifetime worth of suffering. I don't mind if global warming completely destroys life on earth. Life is fucked up!

April 5, 2007

Since I've called Jake before the holiday, I've been feeling happy and thinking more clearly. I'm not caught up in my rage. I can act silly and not feel sad. All I did was talk to him for less than five minutes, but somehow I was affected. As all of this happens, I know I'm doing better emotionally but I'm physically weak. My immune system is very low and my wrists are fragile to injury. My left ankle is also easily sprained. It gets swollen very easily. I haven't been falling asleep till six A.M. the past few nights.

April 12, 2007

I was up all night last night thanks to the Mirapex. I was ready to double dose on clonazepam. I was in a really light sleep and it took me a while to realize I wasn't sleeping. It's weird what these medications do to me. I'm so exhausted today. I had to drink coffee which made me more nervous, but I was able to do the math in class.

April 19, 2007

I had deep dreams last night but they weren't freighting. I woke up laughing. I remember when I first started taking Lyrica, I had deep dreams but they were funny and not frightening. I found that Lyrica also made the anxiety more tolerable.

April 21, 2007

I had nightmares last night. After talking with my mother yesterday about her and my views, I really don't know what's real. People don't really have an ability to understand each other because we don't experience life the same way. I am wondering where my mother's mind is. Has she lost a part of her mind? I don't think she gets what's going on in her own head. I was eating chicken tonight and started thinking about how this chicken's life was short lived. I'm eating it and it doesn't feel right to me. My disgust for sex is more prominent than it has been for a while since I started taking Lyrica. My mother was discussing with me about when she was my age, she went against a way of life which she was told was the correct way. She believes I'm doing the same thing. My mind feels like it's gone.

April 29, 2007

I was feeling agitated throughout most of the day. Tonight I'm feeling very depressed as well. I have had enough of this bullshit life. I'm going on emotional roller coasters and I'm not thinking so sharp. I feel like I'm coming down with something. I'm feeling very horny. When I passed by a girl I tried to smile but it was such a nervous smile that it came out funny. I'm a freak. I'm going to end up alone and miserable for the rest of my life. Even if I have a girl, I will be bored as soon as I get her. Then I'll want to get another girl and the quest will be never-ending.

April 30, 2007

I feel fairly good emotionally. I took a sleeping pill before going to college because I figured I want to be relaxed while taking the psychology test. I was also hoping to start conversations with girls but that didn't happen.

May 7, 2007

I woke up early, around seven A.M., and couldn't fall back asleep. I felt as though I had caffeine. I was feeling agitated today and it was very hard to sit through the whole day of classes. I was feeling extremely nervous with girls being around on campus.

May 29, 2007

My thoughts are intrusive with the thought that humans are not normal; that something isn't right with the human mind. I think about this bear that's being hunted down by humans. What makes our lives more worth living than the bear's? I understand a bear can cause harm to humans, but the blood that gets spilled from humans is the same as mammals'. We're all the same shit. My thoughts overall have been clouded since the beginning of this semester. It's not like last semester where I had moments of clarity in thought. Now I have those moments but they are not as clear. However, I may be more stable emotionally now.

June 4, 2007

I woke up from another deep sleep just now. I can't say it was a nightmare but I do have morbid thoughts as a result from the dream. I dreamt about being at my uncles' house but it was ours. In my dream, I put a chair in a position that it was in prior to us moving in to get a feel of what it was like when my uncles lived there. I was also discussing with my older sister about how there doesn't have to be a plan for each person from a higher power. Look at the uncles that lived in the house—they didn't get married and died single. You can't be passive in this world. You must be aggressive to get what you want. Don't expect any godly intervention because it probably won't happen.

June 6, 2007

I don't feel Dr. Lee is a very good therapist. He isn't so insightful. I feel that he says the wrong things. I only feel he's good as a motivational therapist. I don't want to live this life anymore. It's always the same shit, different day. I don't want to deal with having to eat the same shit every day. I'm tired of sustaining my life. I don't feel I should be living this long. I don't think humans should live this long. I went off the Cymbalta today. I'm thinking of taking more Zoloft so I can drink beer in Barbados so that the headaches I would otherwise get from having alcohol won't be triggered.

June 7, 2007

I went to schedule for fall classes at Kingsborough. My left ankle is so swollen tonight that I couldn't make it to this concert that my father told me about. I was in an overall good mood today but tonight I'm back in a depressed episode. The thought that triggered it was that I'm going to Barbados in less than a month and if I can't get the swelling of my left ankle under control, I won't be enjoying myself much. I envision that my life is going to go on with me ending up in the hospital to get my left ankle treated. This really sucks. Yesterday, I called a girl I met online for the first time. I was very nervous but my anxiety lessened a little overtime. Tonight I'm feeling a great deal of anxiety just being around my family.

June 19, 2007

I went to a healer on Saturday night. I think I'm feeling worse emotionally. Today I'm feeling very depressed. I took a CT scan of my sinuses because they are bothering me and it's the summer. Winter is going to be a blast for me.

June 22, 2007

I'm a little less depressed today. I'm not focused on how messed my life is. I just feel happy for no reason.

June 30, 2007

I'm feeling suicidal. I really want my life to be over with. I feel my life should not have been. I've suffered way too much throughout my life. I see life as a completely meaningless experience. I really hope that something happens to end my life. Life is really fucked up. There is no solution to life's problems. You have a choice to destroy yourself one-way or another and you choose one of them. The whole world is like that. The problem with humans won't be resolved until we are completely destroyed. We will continue to hate and not tolerate others that are not like us. I see a very gloomy future for people and life in general. I had nightmares last night. My left ankle is swollen still and I feel some pain in my wrists. I feel weak. My sinuses are a disaster.

July 9, 2007

Two nights ago after drinking a lot of beer, I went with Mo to his cousin's house and they had weed. I was curious to see how it would affect me. I had a headache from the drinking and the smoking intensified my headache. I've been worrying whether I messed up my emotional balance I received from Jake. I'm going through periods of agitation and uncontrollable worries that I hurt myself by smoking weed. Yesterday, I was feeling upset all day. I hope I didn't fuck things up.

February 2, 2008

I took Adderall tonight to see how it would affect me. I was feeling nervous to begin with but the Adderall may have exacerbated it. I had some moments of confidence but overall it's not worth taking the pill. It didn't help me at my friend's party tonight. I was feeling so nervous even though I took clonazepam. I feel so depressed right now. I want to die. I feel a little less suicidal since I've been speaking with my younger brother but I really wanted to put an end to this life. I still do. Life is bullshit. I can't meet girls because I don't know how to act with them. I try to say things that David D. says but I'm not ready for the challenge of a girl acting upset because of what I said. I told a girl that stopped dancing to dance with me. She didn't want to. So, I said, "What, you're afraid you can't keep up?" She replied that she was keeping up with everyone dancing on the floor. I told another girl, "I'll offer you to suck my cock for $1000". She got very upset and told her friend. I said this because my friend told me I should. I also know I couldn't have her. Her friend told me to apologize and I did. I went back to her after and said, "The offer still stands". I don't know how to interact with women. I can't try to act and say things that don't match who I am. I'm trying to act flirtatious and cocky and it's coming across as insultive.

"To find a girl would take a miracle."

March 16, 2008

I'm sick of this sexual frustration bullshit. I will speak to Dr. S. about using Trelstar. I think that's my best option. My testosterone levels are too high. This is one of the things smoking marijuana did to me. It destroyed my brain. Jake has somehow been able to lessen the extent of it but the sexual urges are still higher than before I started smoking. To find a girl would take a miracle. I cannot wait for that. Besides, how much of a miracle was Jake? It is amazing that he was able to give me my ability to think again but my nightmares are much worse now and harder to control with the meds. The only other option is to go to strip clubs, but I have no one to go with. Also, getting a lap dance and the idea of choosing the dancer causes a great deal of anxiety.

I told my mother about wanting to take Trelstar. She said she really needs to find me a girl. Once a girl knows what I'm about, she wouldn't be interested in me. I want a girl just for physical reasons, mostly. That's the only way I can think of a woman. I couldn't think of her as a friend because my sexual needs are too high. Let my parents try to do the impossible and look for a girl for me. But I doubt their will goes beyond the words, "we really need to find you a girl". I'll take Trelstar and it will relieve at least one part of my miserable and frustrating existence.

May 24 2008

I have been in a state of confusion the past week or so. I don't know what to believe regarding almost everything; from conspiracies of 9/11 to liberal and conservative views. Everything is convincing to me. I don't know if it's because I'm possibly losing my mind. I am feeling really depressed today as I did yesterday. I feel there are too many obstacles to do anything with my life. I can't go over to girls even if it's with the intent of getting rejected. I can't make changes in my life because I get overwhelmed. I'm feeling overwhelmed by everything now. I have a damaged brain and I don't feel there's anything I or anyone else can do to reverse the damage.

July 10, 2008

The past week I've been more intensely suicidal than the past two years. I was searching online for ways to kill myself. The suicidal moods and intense mental pain lifted yesterday night. Now I feel happy and my mind feels stimulated with thought. But I can't sleep at night. I've been up 'till seven A.M. the past four nights. I can't sleep tonight. Dr. S. wants me to continue with the Lunesta.

Part Four

Betrayal

November 1, 2008

I am sick and tired of this bullshit life. I can't stand that my younger sister got with both of my good friends. Now Noah comes over for her and not me. I am left with nothing. No friends I can hang out with nor do I have a girlfriend. Mo won't come over to this house because of my sister cheating on him. Noah practically lives here with her and it eats me up inside, especially right now. I hope this world blows up. I don't want to live anymore. I have no way of meeting a girl or new guys to hang out with. Fuck this bullshit life. I want out of this shit. Why does she have to interfere in my life and fuck shit up? I'm also jealous that Mo has a girl and is happy. It sucks being me. I wish I were dead!

December 12, 2008

I don't know what to do with myself. I scheduled an appointment with the doctor that administers Trelstar. It's an $800 appointment. I would have to take Floxamax with Trelstar because of the risk of possible bone-thinning. I'm feeling overwhelmed about this whole thing. I want to die already. I am really scared about taking this drug. It may also affect my sleep which means it may increase my insomnia and nightmares. My brain is so badly damaged that I don't know if I should do anything else to my body that may damage it more. I want to be rid of my sexual desires. Life fucking sucks so badly. There's way too much pain in life. Noah and my sister are making my life further difficult.

January 3, 2009

I went to a healer that came over to my house for Shabbos. Her name is Lucy. She asked me to visualize a flame in my soul starting small and getting bigger. I was having a very difficult time doing it. I don't think I should continue seeing her. I think it's going to complicate things. She works from a religious angle and I don't want to hear religious shit.

My moods are the same as always. It's a little's worse these days. I get sucked into bad depressive episodes where I feel miserable and there's no end. I finally emerged from it two days ago but it came back last night. It seemed to help to tell Noah that I'm feeling miserable. My depression was lifted just from letting him know. After working with Lucy, I was feeling very nervous and had a bad headache. My headache has lessened after having slept and my mood is stable.

January 9, 2009

I'm really crazy. My mind is so fucked up. I'm coming down with something so I'm having a lot more nightmares. The situation including my younger sister, Noah and me is getting worse. It's bothering me down to my core. I can't stand that Noah comes over to my house to see my sister. The only time I get to see Noah is if he's with her. It's never just with him. At first, she wanted to just hang out with my friends. Then, she gets romantically involved with them. Now, she's serious with Noah and that's ruining my relationship with him. Why can't my friends draw the line when it comes to pursuing a relationship with my sister? At this point, it's fine if they stay together but I shouldn't have to see it every day. I hope I get physically stabbed in my heart!

March 3, 2009

Humans are so off. It seems like whichever process that caused humans to come into existence was not good for the planet. Humans are so screwed up. I don't think humans should have the ability to think. All it does is work for our demise in the end. Humans are overly complicated creatures. It would be better if they seized to exist, especially me. I don't love life. I can't speak to girls or get myself to be sexual. I can't play the game which is designed by nature to get us to reproduce. Being human, to me, is like a human developing cancer. Life living off of a human isn't beneficial to that person. Humans are not beneficial to the planet. I should have been a much simpler life form. This life is completely fucked. Something went really wrong in nature which caused humans to come about. Planet earth is not well.

July 28, 2009

I've been having an increase of obsessive thoughts. I think it may have something to do with taking Vimpat. Maybe it's because I'm lower on the Keppra. I doubt everything from the news and even the Holocaust. How do I know I can trust people's reports on events or history? These thoughts are very intrusive. Noah and my younger sister are upsetting me.

August 6, 2009

Noah and I went to see Dr. Lee yesterday. He tried to express my feelings to Noah while staying objective. At night, Noah said that if I'm a true friend, I wouldn't rat on him to my parents whether he's hanging out with me or not. I told him that if he had spoken to me about this hurt and anger I feel about there being a loss of him as a friend, I wouldn't have had to speak to my parents about it. Noah said as long as I blame my sister for getting involved with my friends, he can't be friends with me. I do feel that they are together now because of me. My sister pursued Noah—she would flirt with him. The first time she saw him, she wanted him.

Regardless, I still feel that if Noah wanted to stay friends with me, he would have found the time to do so. He claims of being busier now and we don't have similar interests. Also, that he is involved in a relationship which just happens to be with my sister. It's all bull. He compared it to his friends that are married: They don't have time to be with him. I know another factor regarding him not hanging out with me: His separation with Mo. Mo kind of held the both of us together. In terms of him being busy now, he could make time for me at least once a week or once every two weeks to sustain our friendship. After all, it does take effort on both parts to sustain a friendship or our friendship will be destroyed. It was.

Now playing make-believe friends, he tries to make an effort to give me more attention. But, this is because I had to confront him and say that I was so distressed with his visits to the house that I wanted to move to the second floor. This had given him some motivation on his part to try to make some effort to hang out with me once in a while—just me and him. Since my father gave him an ultimatum of either being friends with me or finding another place to visit my sister, this has made Noah feel as though he has no choice but to hang out with me. I told him, as not to overwhelm him, that I won't be discussing our relationship with my parents. This is so he shouldn't feel judged if he hasn't hung out with me for a few weeks or even months.

He used to ask me how I was doing and tell me that we're friends so I should tell him what's going on, but not anymore. I know that it must be difficult for him to start a conversation with me since at this point he knows that whatever he's doing with my sister is stressing me out. It doesn't help that he's pursuing a relationship with my sister next door to me. It's constantly in my face. Last night, he came on so strongly and told me that I had no right to blame my sister for getting involved with him. He added that I'm not the cause for their current relationship and that it was Mo that brought them together. That may be true. However, I did play a part in this relationship due to the fact that after the Barbados trip, Noah would come over to my house to see me and after go off to my sister's room. They used this time to get closer to one another. Without this time that he used for coming over to see me to see her, I don't know how far this relationship would have gone.

The only other way he could have pursued a relationship without me being involved would be if he visited Mo and they would meet there. But that wasn't possible due to the circumstance that my sister created by cheating on Mo with some other guy. But the fact is, he did use me to get closer to her and in effect I feel used. I feel betrayed that I wasn't the main reason for him coming over to the house. I know he's not my possession; he doesn't belong to me and is allowed to date my sister. But I feel that he should be more sensitive to what he's doing to me because after all, he has changed things for me. I didn't change things for him. Now I need for him to change the way he lives life for me. Regardless of whether I'm to blame for him growing further away from me, I need him to do something to lessen my distress.

September 24, 2009

I have been by Mo's place for about two weeks. I haven't chosen what I want to do with regards to moving in with Mo. Maybe I'll do it just for the weekend. I had a vision today of my most likely future. I'm going to live at home my whole life just like my uncles did. I'll be there with my older sister and someone else, most likely. This will be my future. I have this feeling in my stomach of anxiety similar to when I wake up after a nightmare or when I have smoked pot. It's a pessimistic outlook on life. There really is no path in my life. I don't feel there's anything out there beyond me in terms of a higher power. Nothing will happen unless I make it happen. I'm not going to meet the people I need to meet in life, like guys or girls similar to me. If Noah breaks up with my sister and moved back home, I'll definitely have a really miserable life on top of my miserable existence—she'll blame me for the breakup. I really hope that my life is cut short somehow. There is no way out.

October 23, 2009

I feel that if Noah were really a friend of mine, he would not have put me through all this and he would have tried to accommodate me by coming over to the house to see my sister less often. If I was into his sister and I saw that coming over to his house to see his sister was disturbing him so much, I would not be able to continue doing that. I wouldn't be able to live with myself. I would try to work out whatever I could to make him feel comfortable. I think he could have gotten a job and an apartment if he were a true friend of mine. Regarding my sister, I don't understand how she could continue to bring him into the house when I asked her repeatedly for some sort of accommodation. There is no room for people like that in my life. I wouldn't want Noah as a friend, being that he can be so insensitive and disrespectful to my feelings and continue to hurt me.

April 20, 2010

Since last Saturday, I've been really agitated and angry. I've been thinking about my sister and Noah a lot. I am overwhelmed with anger towards both of them. I am feeling sick. I feel weak, nauseous and have headaches every day. I'm having very pessimistic thoughts about life. My life is fucked. I will probably not get close to anyone in my life. I will never trust anyone after feeling betrayed by Noah. People are selfish by nature and want to do what's best for them with little or no regard to others. They'll do anything to get what they want, especially if it's their pleasure that's in jeopardy. My psychologist is a young female and is unprofessional. She doesn't seem to have an appreciation for people who suffer the way I do. I don't think she can provide me with the insight I seek. I am so disturbed.

Part Five

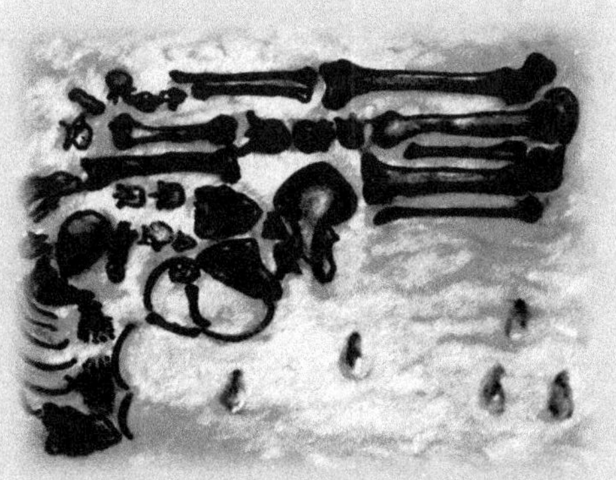

Killing Time

May 3, 2010

I am feeling really horrible lately. I feel miserable more often. I am not fixated on my anger towards my sister and Noah. I'm not fixated on whether what goes on politically is real or not. I am just feeling plain old miserable. All that is on my mind is to study all the time, have no fun and be antisocial because people make me nervous. I can't relate to anyone at bars or parties. So, I'll lock myself up in my room and study. I'll go out when I have to go to school or doctor appointments.

I was on the train and I saw a cute girl. I was thinking how much I would want her. But, realistically, I know that I can't have a cute girl like that because they make me way too nervous and because bitchiness and shallowness often goes along with that look. I just have to think to myself, 'give her ten or twenty more years and her looks are gone. Then what? What pleasure would I have then?' It doesn't seem worth it to get involved with a girl that's not nice when her looks fade away. If I do, I'd be back to the frustrated hell that I'm in now. I'll be twenty-nine and have never gotten involved with a female. It's fucked. It's all fucked up. All there is in life is pain. Pain from losing my ability to drum, pain from losing a friend and feeling betrayed by him, pain from psychotherapy, pain from not being able to bike now because of my back and left ankle, and most of all, the pain of knowing there is no real hope getting out of this mess and that there is only more shit to come.

May 9, 2010

I saw Michelle last week. She is a healer. My insomnia started to get worse three days after seeing her. The difference between this insomnia and the kind I had before is that I've been able to fall asleep pretty much right away but I wake up early and I'm unable to fall back asleep. I have more energy than usual during the day. This goes hand-in-hand with the insomnia where my energy level and mood feel better than usual.

May 21, 2010

I've been having very bad nightmares the past three nights. Some of them were very disturbing. In my dream, there was a cat clawing at my ankles and I was turning in circles trying to get it off and it ripped the skin off my feet. I said to myself, "There goes the skin on my feet". I'm having insomnia as well now. I barely got to sleep Wednesday night and Thursday. Thursday night I felt sleepy but started feeling awake and was up until 5 AM. I feel like Michelle is messing with my fragile balance I had before seeing her. I used to sleep more normally for a while.

My psychologist gave me her opinion on the Noah-Sister dilemma and said that it was completely wrong what they did. Since then, I've been fixated on the anger I feel towards them. I am so angry that Noah betrayed me and that my sister was so selfish as to not think about the consequences of her actions by cheating on Mo and getting involved with Noah. She didn't think about how her actions could affect my social network. I have been selfish with my actions with regards to bothering my youngest sister which caused her suffering. She has every right not to forgive me. It was selfish and she was victimized by me. I was a victim of my sister and I can't let go what she put me through. I can't accept her behavior. To say that I caused my youngest sister suffering does not justify what my other sister put me through. She has not even apologized for her behavior. All she had said was that she's not crazy about her behavior in terms of continuing to bring over Noah even after I begged her to accommodate me in some way.

June 11, 2010

I'm out of my mind. Here I am in this house and I have disgust in the religious way of life. There seems to be something completely wrong with this picture. I should have my own apartment out of this religious community. I'm not normal. The drugs didn't help this situation. I'm feeling this exaggerated feeling of fear that there is something deeply wrong with me. I have repressed emotions. I don't think Michelle could help me anymore than with the temporary relief I get from doing the tapping EFT exercise. This isn't going to be some sort of magical thing like it was with Jake. The thoughts on religion I shared at the Shabbos table felt so warped. I don't even know what I said. I feel I need to be put out. I do not belong in this world. I will never have a friend or girlfriend. I will remain alone because that's the way it needs to be. I can't have people in my life. People only end up disappointing me and I end up becoming dysfunctional over it, like I did with Noah and my sister. I don't feel any trust towards people. I realize I should never have been friends with Mo or Noah.

August 7, 2010

The strangest thing happened last night. When I asked a friend of the family, Frank, to pass something on the table, he did it very quickly and uncontrolled. Later on, I was by his side of the table and was reaching for something and he suddenly jerked out of his chair and went into the kitchen. I think that something deep and profound was going on. My mother and a friend of hers, Jen, according to Frank, had a mother-daughter relationship in a previous life. Also, according to Frank, my older sister was his sister in a past life. I think I may have played a role in Frank's past life event that he has yet to work out. This world is so strange! I wouldn't be surprised if something did indeed happen. Even if it's not real, it's real in Frank's mind. Or, maybe it is real. Just as unbelievable as it may sound, Jake did have some healing effect on me. For someone else who had not experienced a similar thing, hearing it might lead that person to believe it was all psychological; I believed that it would work and so it did. Everything may be real in Frank's mind or maybe he's just nuts like Dr. M. A similar reaction of being uncontrolled occurred with Dr. M. when he drove me to the train station. I wasn't projecting as he claimed I was. He really was uncontrollably nervous.

August 8, 2010

Dr. M. and the drugs, i.e., marijuana, really made me crazy. The thing that probably makes Frank so repulsed by me is my continuous thoughts of how God is evil, how life sucks and how religion is bullshit. I always try to tell my mother these thoughts and I share it with almost everyone. I have gone mad and that is for certain. I'm not the only one in the family's that has lost it. My eldest sister is pretty disturbed as well as my other sister and younger brother. When I got into a conversation about religion, God and Allah, I didn't know how to control myself from going on and talking about it. I kind of lose myself. Sometimes I share these thoughts with strangers or guests. I was sharing these thoughts with one guest that was over at the house, mostly because I feel the person's nuts himself. I should go downstairs Friday nights and not say anything.

November 2, 2010

I've been fixated on distressing thoughts about whether the things that are reported on the news are really true. For example, I wonder if the senator running for the Senate seat is really running or it's just being shown on TV and is not true. I'm feeling confused about whether I believe that things are just random or whether there's some intervention from a higher power. I think I may need some more of this medication. I finally got over my sinusitis which got infected twice. Even after the second treatment of antibiotics, I still felt sinus pressure. I started using the steam inhaler and that has seemed to finally stop the sinusitis from getting infected again. I spoke to Noah about the worry I have about never being able to get over my anger with him or my sister. Ever since then I have not been as distressed thinking about it. I get upset at times but I don't get fixated to the point where I can't function. Noah came to eat for a Friday night dinner and it was difficult but manageable. It started to upset me when they were holding hands at the table. I couldn't deal with that. At least I'm not so distressed over them. I have thoughts about technology that it ought not to be this way; it's unnatural the way humans fight nature's cold temperatures by using a heater. Maybe my thoughts are more distressful because of the pressure about the IT exams I need to take.

December 30, 2010

I have a problem with Sally, a psychologist I was referred to in the clinic. She had mentioned that she was going to discuss my case with her supervisor. So, the next week I asked her what the supervisor said but she had not spoken to him yet. I asked her if I could speak with him to see whether he could shed some light on my problems. She said that she shouldn't have told me that she was discussing my case with her supervisor because I should have total confidence with her. I responded, "It's not like I haven't doubted your therapy before you mentioned your discussion you were to have with your supervisor". I went on further to say that her lack of professionalism keeps me from having respect for her therapy. Case in point, when I mentioned that her patient that came out of her office really was cute she responded by saying she's beautiful inside and out. When she said that, I told her that it was unprofessional to say that.

She responded by saying, "What do you want me to say? She's not pretty?"

The response itself is unprofessional in my opinion. She tends to just speak her mind without filtering out certain things which makes me see her in the same light as when I'm discussing my issues with my sister. I told her that I thought she was unprofessional.

She became flushed, "Whoo. Okay".

I felt bad because she seemed upset. I apologized to her and said, "If I offended you, I'm sorry".

"You're projecting", she said. "I'm not upset". I kept on apologizing. She told me that I need to learn people skills.

The next week she said that she was upset because here she was working really hard with me and I was questioning her therapy. She mentioned the reason why she said I was projecting. It was because she tends to do that when a situation gets intense and she says things to lighten up the situation. She went on to say that she feels like I am always comparing her to Dr. M. and don't respect her opinion as a therapist. Also, if I wanted, she could recommend someone who she thinks is insightful while I work with her solely on people skills. Or, I can continue working with her. She added that she's concerned about me going from one therapist to another because no one in life is perfect and it would be therapeutic if I can work out my issues with her and accept that she has faults and is not going to be like Dr. M.

I really don't know what I want at this point. On the one hand, I want a therapist I can speak to so I can gain the skills to speak with someone and have some kind of social contact outside of my family. On the other hand, I want a kind of therapy that I could probably only get from an expensive therapist. And I don't know if it's worth it. Do I want the insight that Dr. M. has been providing me because I want to be entertained by its thought-provoking qualities? I do think I pretty much have lost respect for Sally. I think she has some good ideas for me or some knowledge to share with me. I think I have grown because when I first came to see her, I found it overwhelming just to make a cup of tea. When she told me I should go make a cup of tea, I did. Now, I'll make a cup of tea with no problem.

I have finished vocational training with taking the A+ and Network+ exams and passed them. I feel that I got this far because I have this philosophy that if I can't kill myself then I want to be really busy so that time will go by faster and before I know it I'll be old and dead. The stress produced from the computer training and from taking the exams happened to not have gotten the best of me—not to the point where I could no longer function.

I think I was provocative with Sally with the way I came across. I decided I was going to tell her straight up how I felt about the way she conducts therapy. I found her to be a little provocative because she was wearing makeup. It did come out as more of an attack I think. I'm also stressed out because of the exams and had been manipulated by a stranger who asked me for money on the train who convinced me to go with him to the bank to take out $200 from my account. This guy claimed to be from Israel and told me he has currency only in the form of NIS (New Israeli Shekel) and it couldn't be exchanged at the bank since he didn't have an account with them. I wasn't clear what he wanted and I went out of that train station thinking that he only wanted to exchange NIS to USD. He said that he wanted to borrow money from me after we got out of the train station and that he would pay me back by mail. Anyway, I felt stupid for falling for it. He made me feel united as Jews and as one people and I wanted to help.

January 28 2011

I've started taking Mirtazapine, generic for Remeron, 15 mg.

January 29, 2011

I stopped taking Remeron. It made me feel flu-like symptoms. I felt weak and horrible. My mouth was very dry and I slept all day until I wasn't feeling weak, which was around 8 PM.

February 2, 2011

I started taking Remeron 7.5 mg.

March 8, 2011

My mood is wrecked. I have been feeling sick on and off for three weeks now. I've been avoiding dairy foods but today I decided: Fuck it I am not getting better and unless this weakness and nausea is due to the medication, then I have the flu. I'm feeling really agitated. I only got six hours of sleep last night. I got myself to go to the library to study so that made me feel happy. Overall, I feel pretty miserable. I have a lot of mental anguish, doubts and feelings of helplessness. I had one day last week where I felt focused and happy, more than I have before I started taking Remeron. My mother wants a rabbi to come to the house to speak with the family about religion. It's very insensitive of my mother to put me in the position of dealing with the anger I have towards religion. This event will stir up my emotions. I think she's completely out of touch. With my mood fragile as it is, why should she put something in my face that could throw me off?

June 4, 2011

I feel like shit. I've come down with something. I'm not feeling clear minded. I feel depressed and I want out of this hellish existence. With my IT internship, my back goes out very easily. I'm so screwed. I'm going to wind up alone and bitter for the rest of this godforsaken life. I have had some good days since taking Remeron. I've been taking vitamins that have prevented me from getting sick as often as I did.

September 11, 2011

I stopped taking Remeron Friday night. I was developing a fever again. I had enough of this. I didn't even speak to my psychiatrist first. I wasn't thinking so clearly yesterday.

September 29, 2011

I'm still getting sick constantly. The symptoms of the virus are not as severe as when I was on Remeron. I am getting a sore throat repeatedly. My throat finally felt like it was getting better yesterday but today it hurts again. I'm not weak all the time like I was when I was taking Remeron. If I drink milk in the morning, I barely have enough energy to take a shower. Something is very off with my immune system. I hope the Remeron didn't fuck it up further. My insomnia is bad since I stopped taking the Remeron. I fall asleep okay as long as I take 1 mg of Klonopin but wake up to go to the bathroom at 5 AM and can't fall back asleep.

October 6, 2011

I keep getting sick even though I stopped the Remeron. However, I'm able to function and study more than when I was on the Remeron. I am getting repeated viruses and sore throats. The doubting thoughts of whether the president is really in the White House or whether the news being reported on TV can be trusted have not surfaced (like they were when I was on the Vimpat prior to taking the Remeron). I believe that the Remeron's subduing effect on my doubts about the president's and news' authenticities still lasted months after having ended its dose. My insomnia is terrible. My dreams are very deep.

Sometimes they're disturbing but more or less, my dreams are very deep and vivid.

November 2, 2011

Amazingly, I have not been getting sick in the past few weeks. The repeated sore throat seems to have subsided. I still have a cold though. My insomnia is bad. I fall asleep about two or three A.M. Then, I wake up to go to the bathroom at five or six A.M. and can't fall back asleep.

November 17, 2011

I stopped taking Lyrica. My insomnia has been a little better since I took the CCNA exam. I have not been getting unusually sick. I got sick twice this month and took vitamin D3 2000 units for one day and I feel a little better today.

November 20, 2011

Note to myself about what to tell the healer, Stacey:

Since seeing Jake, I've been doing better in terms of clarity in thought. After a few years of having more days of clarity in thought, I started noticing my immune system had been compromised and I got sick very often. Any pre-existing issues like my weakened left ankle and tendinitis in my left wrist took longer to heal and I got hurt more easily. My sinuses get more inflamed especially during the winter months and I have to use a nasal spray almost all year round to control my sinus pressure. My nightmares that started ever since I stopped smoking cold turkey are harder to control now with the meds and are coupled with insomnia. The medication used to control the nightmares before seeing Jake.

Overall, my emotional and mental states are very fragile. My emotional stability can be thrown off easily if I have an alcoholic beverage or if there's any change in my environment. My mood is definitely better since seeing Jake. I am happier more often now than three years ago. I mostly feel hopeless in life and my goal in life is to do whatever I can to pass the time so my life can be over before I know it.

I feel I have aged thirty years in the past ten years. My back goes out just from riding my bike. My neck goes out from my nightmares while sleeping on my side. I often forget just how hopeless things are and feel happy for no reason.

Do you think there seems to be a trade-off from seeing Jake? Will seeing you cause adverse effects? Two healers I went to in the past threw me off balance and worsened my insomnia and nightmares. With one healer, it took three to six months to regain some balance.

March 26, 2012

I have been working since the last week of January. I just love that almost two months of my life has gone by quickly. I don't like it here and I want out. The only thing I can do are things that will make life feel like it's going by quicker. I feel hopeless physically, emotionally and sexually. I think it's a rationalization to think it's good that I'm so paralyzed by the fear of girls so I don't wind up in a relationship; all of which will overwhelm me and lead to the girl wanting marriage and children. It will result in heartbreak for both me and the girl because we will be on different paths, philosophically. I keep thinking this because I imagine it reduces the frustration that I don't have a girl. I'm still very frustrated but I think that having a girlfriend is like having a drug. At first it's exciting but when that initial excitement diminishes, I will be back to square one. I want a permanent solution to this temporary problem. Saying 'hello' to a girl is not going to necessarily lead to a relationship, marriage and kids. If I just make small talk with a girl, it won't last very long because I don't know how to flirt or play games. I don't know why, in my mind, I'm jumping from the idea of meeting a girl to marriage and children. Maybe it's because I was raised with this way of thinking. Most likely all religious girls in my community are thinking along the same lines.

March 27, 2012

I have been off of antibiotics for ten days and I already need it again. I need to take it for a bad sore throat. I need to take two pills of Omnicef twice a day for two days. My immune system is severely fucked. I'm taking probiotics this time.

April 7, 2012

I started taking Pristiq 50 mg. I had a headache today. I don't know if it was related to the Pristiq. I started taking 2000 units of vitamin D3.

April 9, 2012

I feel weak and nauseous during work especially after I had cheese with pitta bread. I feel like I have a fever after my shower. I don't know if work is bad for me. There is a lot of dust and I don't know if it is contributing to me getting sick so often this past month. I was on antibiotics twice this month.

April 12, 2012

I had really bad nightmares last night. I don't know if it's due to my new medication or because of the stress of my job. The bosses are not happy with my performance at work and it's affecting my self-worth. Yesterday, the boss told my coworker, "So, it's not worth having him work here". I think I'll time myself how long it takes to do the auction and tell them this is how long it takes me. If it doesn't suffice, then I'm not the right fit for this job. I may be more vulnerable to the drama at work because of this new medication.

April 18, 2012

I've been feeling overall more relaxed this past week. When I walk down the street, I don't get as nervous walking by people. I am getting sick again even though I am taking 2500 units of vitamin D3. My throat feels irritated. I have a terrible headache today partly due to my TMJ. Last night's dreams were very intense and I was clenching my teeth really bad.

August 9, 2012

I saw the healer, Stacey, twice. Since I made a phone call to her, my nightmares have gotten more intense and disturbing. I also got sick the same time. That may also have contributed to the nightmares. I have been sick nonstop. I get viruses one after the other. This happens until eventually I am prescribed antibiotics by Dr. F. I find that if I feel weak when I wake up and sit out in the sun for fifteen to twenty minutes, I feel energetic and am able to take a shower. But once I eat dairy, the weakness comes on again. I get fevers occasionally as well. The day after I saw Stacey, I was having a fever at night and the following day. The fever went away but the weakness remained. When Stacey was working on me, I could feel a wave of energy through my body similar to when Jake was working on me.

I have a theory as to why I've been getting sick continuously. I think the Remeron triggered an immune system problem which is a malabsorption of vitamin D3. At first, when I was taking the Remeron, I felt like I was getting sick repeatedly after a week of taking it. Then, I had blood work and it showed my vitamin D levels were low. Dr. F. told me to supplement with vitamin D3. Almost instantly there was a difference. I wasn't getting sick anymore. I thought I was in the clear. I had blood work done again and my vitamin D3 levels were normal. Dr. F. then told me to stop taking the vitamin D3. I stopped taking it and the next day or so I was getting sick again with fevers and sore throat. So, I started taking vitamin D again, however, this time it doesn't seem to be cutting it. I was taking 2000 units of vitamin D3 and my blood work showed that I had low levels of D3. Dr. F. told me to keep doing what I'm doing. I think my body is not absorbing D3 from a pill but only from the sun. I am now taking 3000 units of D3. I'll see if that makes a difference. I am hoping Stacey can help me with this.

I had deep dreams last night. I dreamt that I was in the year 1998. I was with my family at the dinner table. I was telling my family about 9/11 and that the twin towers will be destroyed. I explained that it was all to finish the job the terrorists started with the towers in '93. I told everyone to go and visit the twin towers because it will no longer be there. I told my older brother about the relationships of the family—Noah and my sister and my oldest sister and her boyfriend. Of course, he didn't believe me. I told him that Mo became a friend of mine and Noah came over to the house to eventually start pursuing a relationship with my younger sister. I told everyone that we will get a cat and that my father will be the most attached to it. I was looking at my file and it stated which school I was currently attending. I said, "I can no longer go there you have to get me out of this school with my high school principal".

I have a sore throat today, probably from waiting in Dr. F.'s office for two hours. I don't feel optimistic about Stacey's healing.

August 27, 2012

I saw Stacey today. I did not feel better from her visit. I am feeling weak lately and stuck. I can't study. I hope this all doesn't turn to shit and that I'll need Jake to make things the way they were, which was not all that great. I would like to get rid of my nightmares and insomnia but they are worse since seeing Stacey. I feel confused and I am not able to clarify my thoughts. My insomnia is, however, under control while taking hydroxyzine.

September 17, 2012

My left ankle has swollen up quite a bit. I feel life is such bullshit. The difficulties I have in life are ridiculous. This is a fucked up world for me. My anxiety is so high that I can't play piano in front of people. I am so fearful of girls my age. It's just fucked. Stacy doesn't seem to have had a lasting effect on me. I am doing physical therapy for my left ankle and that's making me more vulnerable too. All I did was walk to Prospect Park and my left ankle got sprained.

September 18, 2012

I don't feel like taking antibiotics. The problem might be bacterial or strep. If I could die, it wouldn't be so bad. There is not much prospect for a positive future for me. I'm ruined. The reason I get so agitated when I have a bacterial infection is because of smoking marijuana. I'm damaged goods. I have to live a life with a compromised immune system, nightmares, neck problem, wrist problems and left ankle problems. But mostly, it's the problem with my brain that I don't want to deal with. I don't want to live a life with the prospect of not having a girlfriend due to my anxiety.

September 19, 2012

My sinuses have flared up. I have some kind of infection. I feel weak and irritable. My neck is the worst it has been in a while. My nightmares have been worse the past two days. My mood improved immediately after I left a message on Stacy's answering machine yesterday. This was her office number, not her personal number. I would like to fight this sinus infection on my own.

September 22, 2012

It hasn't even been a month since I've stopped taking antibiotics and I feel I might need it again. My mood is so bad, I can't talk to anyone. I left my window open at night and woke up with a sore throat. I had very bad nightmares last night and my neck had a bad spasm. My left ankle is swollen. I want out of this fucking life. I have no passions in life. All I do is study for my exams and look for a future of work in computer repair.

September 23, 2012

I have been taking Singulair the past few days. I feel like it has helped relieve my sinus pressure and possibly avoided the development of a sinus infection—in which case I would need antibiotics. Lately, I find that I can articulate better. My neck is out, though. This hasn't happened in quite some time regardless of my nightmares being so intense.

September 25, 2012

I am feeling in an overall good mood. My throat hurts. It seems I came down with another virus or it's a continuation of the virus I had last week. I feel very articulate and sociable.

September 28, 2012

My infection has gotten worse. Now I have green mucus. My sinuses have not been affected too much because I'm taking Singulair. My dreams are very vivid and my insomnia is somewhat bad.

October 9 2012

I started taking Omnicef on my own. The reason for this is because I have been feeling sick for the past three weeks. First, my sinuses were being attacked (now they're alleviated). Then, I felt bumps in the back of my throat. My nightmares are very intense. It's only been a little over a month the last time I took antibiotics.

October 13, 2012

The Omnicef isn't helping. Maybe I should just let nature take its course—without the Omnicef. I wish I had the balls to just stop the Omnicef and let what's coming to me, come. I'm ready to give up life even with all my possessions. I don't care. My body can't fight for shit since I saw Jake and taking Remeron. I am ready to let go of life.

October 15, 2012

I went on a boat cruise yesterday. I took two propranolol 20 mg. I felt really upset afterwards. I am so upset that I can't speak to girls. I didn't feel social and I couldn't wait until it was over. I approached maybe two or three girls. I feel there is no hope of finding a girl. Even if I do find a girl, it won't be the end of my misery. I feel castration is the only answer right now. I feel very depressed today. I want to die already.

October 22, 2012

I went to Dr. F. and he diagnosed what was on the back of my throat. He told me that they are stones and might have puss behind them and that I should take another antibiotic. There is no way I am going to take another antibiotic when I've been taking it for almost two weeks. He touched my outer lip with his otoscope again.

October 28 2012

I have a really bad headache tonight. My throat is probably really red and infected and I probably need antibiotics again. Even though I raised my daily vitamin D to 4000 units, I'm still sick. I felt pretty good over the weekend. I felt really happy and hyped up and was acting very silly. I associated this to the high dose of vitamin D3 I'm taking. My nightmares are pretty intense. They are very deep and disturbing.

November 11, 2012

I got some sun even though it's later in the fall. I was in the sun for an hour with not gaining much of a tan. I was feeling somewhat depressed and was going to watch The Butterfly Effect but couldn't find the movie. I felt as though I was falling into a depression and decided I wanted to reflect on all the pain I have been through and how meaningless my life has been. I am feeling less depressed now.

November 26, 2012

I slept by Mo's for three nights. I came home during my stay. Each time I would come home, I felt depressed. When I got back to Mo's, I felt better. Now I am home and I'm stuck in a bad depression. I want to end this life. I'll look into taking cyanide.

December 2, 2012

I went to my therapist, Sam, and I wasn't thinking clearly. I was talking to him about taking cyanide and he mentioned that if this is a topic I am going to bring up, eventually he'll be liable to report. I told him I am not capable of going through with suicide.

December 16, 2012

After eating breakfast, I was considering driving to the tanning salon to get rid of my weakness but then I noticed I wasn't feeling that weak due to the adrenaline rush I got from the thought of going. This makes it seem like the weakness has a psychological component, but there is a physiological factor, too (chronic fatigue syndrome). A similar reaction, in regards to its psychological factor, happened when I was taking Zyprexa, which side effect made me weak. The weakness I felt would become more severe from psychological factors such as increased stress levels.

Part Six

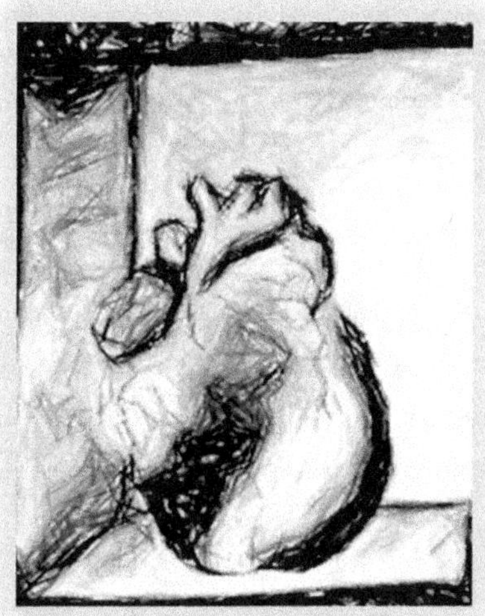

Dating

December 24, 2012

When I'm in public, I feel like my lips are sealed. I can't say anything to strangers. I don't know how I am going to go through the boot camp for approach anxiety.

January 2, 2013

I had full-fledged nightmares last night. I dreamt that I was in confrontation with the family. I was hitting my oldest brother and my father in their mouths. There was so much anger. My life is so fucked. Who knows what's in store for this world?

January 13, 2013

My anxiety was really high most of the day. I went to the dating coach boot camp last night and it was torture to approach women. I am feeling less anxious tonight. I texted one of the girls I approached in a group last night. I'm feeling focused and have clarity in thought.

January 19, 2013

I went on a date with a girl I met at a speed dating event. I wasn't really nervous and she wasn't the least bit provocative. I didn't find her attractive. She wasn't repulsive though. I went out later that night with the dating coach, Christopher, to eat. After, his associate, Jerry, and I went to a birthday party. I was very nervous when talking to girls. Jerry encouraged me to speak to some girls, so I did. I had a bad headache that night. On my way home, I was feeling very pessimistic about life and was listening to Tunnel Trance Force.

January 20, 2013

I am feeling depressed. I had disturbing dreams about Dr. F. He was checking my throat and nose. Upon finishing, he said that nothing was wrong with me. I told him I feel the beginning of sinus irritation. He became angry and left the otoscope in my mouth and I was holding it to prevent it from falling. Christopher was there, too. There was so much anger directed at me. My brain is really fucked up.

January 25, 2013

I didn't have nightmares like I thought I would last night because I stopped taking Vimpat. I've been getting more tension/sinus headaches. I went out with Jerry and I practiced approaching girls. That caused a great deal of anxiety. The anxiety lessoned after repeated approaches. I got two numbers.

January 26, 2013

I had insomnia last night. I woke up at 6 A.M. and couldn't fall back asleep until 9 A.M. Tonight was a disaster. I went to numerous bars with Jerry. I found myself very much in my own head and could barely make conversation with girls. There were a lot of attractive females there. I fucking need one and I don't feel that Christopher's approach to picking up girls is authentic and my anxiety is too high for me to keep faking it.

My anxiety didn't lessen that much even after repeated exposure to women.

February 2, 2013

My anxiety was fairly manageable when approaching girls in Whole Foods.

February 4, 2013

I feel like I'm coming down with something again. I have weakness and nausea. It's on and off. My mood is not good and I feel really depressed. I've had enough of this frustration about being unable to meet a girl. Torture. That's what it's all about.

February 7, 2013

I was feeling weak this morning. I had more energy after I ate dark chocolate. My throat hurts. I watched The Butterfly Effect (2004) last night and cried a lot. My dreams are intense but tolerable.

February 9, 2013

I started taking Omnicef.

February 12, 2013

I'm feeling much better today. I had energy to bike as well as do my back exercises. I have been thinking about another way to describe my perception of life: I'm a coward. I don't go through life with the attitude that I'm going to attack this challenge. Instead, I take on challenges in life because choosing to do nothing is difficult. Doing something is also difficult but it kills time. My attitude towards life is so bleak.

February 17, 2013

I went to a singles event with Jerry. I didn't feel much nervousness when approaching women. I felt a little nervous but it wasn't too bad. I approached the same girl twice during the night. I forgot which people I approached. Not only do I forget names but I forget faces that I see for only short periods of time.

February 19, 2013

I had major nightmares last night. I was being confronted by everyone in the family. My father and others were involved. Yesterday, my older sister got really angry that I ate her food and that is what probably fueled the nightmares. I went to Workforce1 to try to apply for training in Windows Server. I almost approached two girls at Starbucks today; however, I had a headache.

February 23, 2013

I started feeling weak after I ate dinner. After I took a shower I felt really tired and weak. I slept and I had very deep dreams. I'm still sick. The antibiotics may not be helping me fully recover from this infection due to my body's resistance to Omnicef.

February 26, 2013

I was able to approach a girl in Starbucks and said the pickup line of, "Are you into fashion?" I am glad I was able to do that. Later, another girl was in Starbucks but I couldn't get myself to say anything. She wasn't wearing clothes I felt I could comment on.

February 28, 2013

I fell into a deep depression after talking to my youngest sister about my dreams last night. I dreamt that my high school principal gave me two-hundred dollars. I didn't see him as someone I should have been afraid of. Due to my mood, I watched An American Crime (2007). I could relate to the emotional hell that one of the victims went through in terms of fear, not the physical abuse. I know what it's like to be caught up in that hell.

March 1, 2013

My throat is hurting really bad. I started myself on Suprax. I am tired of constantly getting sick. I am not thinking so clearly today. My sinuses have not gotten completely better since the last infection. It seems most likely that my body has resistance to Omnicef.

March 2, 2013

I was feeling pretty down most of the day. I went out with the dating crew and my anxiety was really high. I wasn't in the greatest mood due to the antibiotics. I am glad time seems to be going by really fast. Before I know it I'll be dead and there will be no more talk of me being sexually frustrated. YAY!

March 6, 2013

My headache was excruciating. I went to sleep during the day and had very deep dreams. My throat has white puss in the back. I am not thinking as clearly at times during the day. I fear that the infection I have is resistant to antibiotics. I've been on antibiotics for a month now. I may have caught a mutated form of a throat infection which is resistant to traditional antibiotics.

March 11, 2013

I'm still sick. I'm feeling weakness. Even after I took a nap I felt weak at times. My throat hurts. I feel negative about life and the fact that my immune system is compromised.

March 14, 2013

I stopped taking Suprax. I had a couple of pieces of dark chocolate and that gave me energy. It also made me feel jittery. I'm feeling really hopeless. My throat is hurting on the left side and there is some puss. If I get sicker, I'll get some tests done to find out what kind of bacteria I have and get it treated. I'm tired of this whole thing. Maybe I should just let nature take its course and let the living thing inside me kill its host.

March 16, 2013

I went out with the dating coach tonight. I took one Klonopin and another before I left the house. My headache started kicking in and couldn't control it even with the Sumatriptan and Advil. I took three Klonopin's today plus one tonight. I got a number from a girl I'm not attracted to.

"To be real with women or not to be, that is the question."

March 22, 2013

I went to a singles event with Jerry and I got two women's numbers both of whom are psychiatrists. I'm not crazy about Jerry's approach toward communicating with women. I feel that it's not genuine when I speak, more or less, bullshit. To be real with women or not to be, that is the question.

March 27, 2013

In the afternoon, my headache started kicking in. I think it started after calling all three girls that I met at Hudson Terrace. I left a voicemail on each of the girls' phones.

April 4, 2013

I approached an attractive girl in Starbucks. She was sitting next to me and I commented on her boots. It was a positive interaction. She kept on yapping away.

April 12, 2013

I am feeling very depressed since yesterday from working with the dating coach last night. He was hard on me and told me to ask myself, 'what can I do in a situation where I have nothing else to say?' instead of telling myself that I don't know what to do in a situation. This depression has got quite a hold on me.

April 18, 2013

After I took a hot bath, I felt faint and very weak. I took a nap and the weakness subsided but worsened later this evening. I hate this fatigue shit. My mind hasn't been clear since the fatigue has started up.

April 19, 2013

I had some dark chocolate because I was feeling a little weak. I felt less weak after I did my leg lifts with weights and side to side stretches. Also, I went out in the sun for twenty minutes and after that I had a lot of energy and I was thinking clearly. I went out tonight to the Gansevoort and practiced remembering girls' names. I went up to them, asked for their names and then left. Jerry wanted me to ask for the girls' names and where they live and write it down afterward.

May 6, 2013

I went out with a girl yesterday along with her friends. I held her hand while walking but I felt really uncomfortable, so I let it go. I am not attracted to this girl. I was, however, attracted to one of her friends.

I told Christopher, the dating coach, to bring girls to the next class so I could practice touching girls. He brought two girls on Saturday. One of them, I thought, was really cute. We went to the club together and the girl I thought was cute sat on Larry's lap. Larry is another person in my dating class. I was so turned on by that. I couldn't function anymore. I was so jealous and it caused a lot of mental anguish. I don't want to experience that pain again. It's way too much. I had two beers and had a pleasant high. I opened multiple sets of girls with no openers. I would prefer to do it that way. I was speaking to a girl for a long time. This girl was part of one of the groups I approached. I was not attracted to her, though. I was really depressed when I came home Saturday night. I just wanted to die. I still want out. I don't feel I'm cut out for this game of attraction.

May 8, 2013

I've been sick since Monday. I have a sore throat and weakness. I feel quite depressed and that life is completely fucked for me with my compromised immune system and emotional instability. I got really fucked over by the marijuana and the fucking healers.

May 16, 2013

I started taking Ciprofloxacin.

May 17, 2013

I stopped taking Ciprofloxacin. I had crazy nightmares last night. I started taking Suprax.

May 20, 2013

I am feeling much better today. I am much less weak and I worked out on the bike. It's been two weeks since I did because I was sick. My mood is okay. The Cold and Flu Formula really helped reduce the severity of the symptoms of this bacterial infection. I think I should take it every day since I'm always getting sick.

May 22, 2013

I went to Starbucks but I couldn't speak to any girls. I don't have the balls to say things like, 'that watch is cool', or, 'you look like you're into fashion'. Maybe it's the fear of a girl knowing that I'm attracted to her. But mostly, I don't feel it's appropriate to approach strangers.

June 3, 2013

I have a fever tonight. I'm still getting sick. I'm taking the Cold and Flu Formula three times a day now. I feel more clarity in thought. I'm so overwhelmed to speak to girls with the method in which it is necessary to spark attraction with them. I hate that I'm not naturally that person who is cocky and funny.

I want out of this fucked up world. I'm so frustrated with not having a girl.

June 9, 2013

I felt really good today. I had no weakness. Even after I had a frozen yogurt, I didn't feel weak. I can articulate well. It definitely seems like the Cold and Flu Formula is helping my immune system.

June 12, 2013

I went to the improv class tonight and I was very tense. I disliked most of the exercises. The class consisted of mostly girls and some of them are attractive. I can't take it. I don't want to deal with approaching girls anymore. It causes too much anxiety. I think I should just get a job and stay busy because this torture is here to stay. I would love to be chemically castrated. I should first try working. I can't take this sexual frustration. I just need to die.

October 23, 2013

I saw Dr. R. and he said I may have a virus that doesn't go away. I started taking Cold and Flu Formula three times a day using half the dose of what I normally use. I've been having insomnia since I've been going down on the Zoloft.

November 30, 2013

I started taking Wellbutrin.

December 6, 2013

I stopped taking the Wellbutrin. I was feeling flu-like symptoms today. I didn't have enough energy to take a shower.

December 7, 2013

I took 2 mg of Klonopin and 50 mg of hydroxyzine before I went to a speed dating event. I felt pretty calm. I didn't feel comfortable when we all met downstairs after the event. It is a lot easier talking to girls at a speed dating event because it's one on one. Approaching girls in groups is too intense.

December 12, 2013

When I gargled with saltwater three times a day, prior to taking the Wellbutrin, I was able to control my fatigue symptom and wasn't getting sick. When I had sugar, I would feel weak. Now, after taking Wellbutrin, albeit having stopped it, I feel fatigue. There is no direct correlation anymore between having sugar and feeling weak afterward. My weakness is persistent now. It seems I have yet again hurt my immune system by trying this drug. My insomnia is also much worse after having stopped taking Wellbutrin. I need to take 100 mg of hydroxyzine as opposed to the previous dose of 25 mg at night.

December 25, 2013

I watched The Butterfly Effect (2004). I feel depressed now. I'm also feeling sad because Sherry says that I am perfect for her and that the ball is in my park. It's up to me whether I want to have a serious relationship with her or not. But I don't.

She doesn't turn me on much. What's this fucking life for anyway? I don't want to procreate. Sherry is just not enough and I feel bad about it. Fuck!

December 28, 2013

I had my exam today. I'm MCITP certified.

January 2, 2014

I went out with Sherry to a New Year's Eve party. She started kissing a guy. I felt jealous that I can't get with a girl and she always gets with a guy. I get way too fucking nervous around girls. I was drenched with insecurity while talking with an attractive girl. It seemed like she was attracted to me, too, but I couldn't even manage to buy her a drink. When Sherry kissed the guy at 12 A.M., I felt like crying. I felt sad the next day as well.

January 4, 2014

I went out with Sherry and her friend to a karaoke place. I spoke to a girl there and got her number. She was kind of cute but I wasn't too crazy about her personality. She came across defensive at times or what felt to be a sort of attack.

January 5, 2014

The girl that I met last night at the Watering Hole texted me back. I will call her Wednesday.

January 12, 2014

I met with Alyssa in the city. She is somewhat cute, although she doesn't care too much with how she looks. She's petite, so that's good, but she has a hard shell. She's tough and somewhat sarcastic. She was laughing at all of the things I said. She probably likes me, but I'm not sure if as a friend or something more. She smokes cigarettes. I'm not too crazy about that.

January 13, 2014

I went with Sherry to Hudson Terrace Friday night. There were so many girls and I didn't approach even one. I was nervous to the fucked degree. I give up on this whole thing. I'm way too nervous in these club environments. Nuke this world!

January 17, 2014

I feel a little sad about Sherry. She told me over the phone that she loves me. What am I supposed to do? I feel bad for her and at the same time I'm thinking I could have this great girl that could love me. It's nice and all but what about my sexual frustration? The thing is, I probably won't meet anyone else.

January 18, 2014

Sherry came over to my house to eat. I am feeling extremely depressed and agitated. She must have set me off. I can't talk to anyone. I just want to die. I really don't care about anything. If I can't have the girl that I'm actually attracted to then

I wish I could run into an electric fence. I'm going to have to live in mental agony like this. I can't get a girl I truly desire because of my fucking anxiety. Death sounds like a sweet deal right now. Fuck!

January 20, 2014

John, my father's friend, told me that the humane thing to do with Sherry is to not see her till April of this year to assess how I feel about her. He doesn't think I should continue seeing her since I don't want kids and she does. Also, I don't envision myself being with her in the future.

January 31, 2014

I've been depressed the past few days. I am having intense mental anguish, agitation and difficulty relating to family members. I don't want to be around anyone. I am still sick with this virus or flu. I feel very weak. My sinuses are irritated. I may also be depressed due to Sherry. Yesterday, I told her that one of the thoughts I have associated with this depression is that I don't think I can get woman my age without charisma. I'm too nervous around women. I'm not a smooth talker. I'm too uptight and women don't like that. It ultimately doesn't matter if I look good. What matters is having a bullshit character. I basically told Sherry, in not so many words, that I want someone better for myself. I didn't filter the words I said to her because I was feeling miserable.

February 2, 2014

I feel sad about Sherry. It's a real shame. I will lose her because I'm too shallow and want a cute girl. She could do, but I won't get exactly what I want in a physical relationship. I am going to encourage her to keep meeting other men. I like her and care for her well-being. I'm definitely more attracted to her than I was when I first met her. I just really want a girl that will take my breath away. But that's asking too much. Most girls don't like guys like me. I'm like an alien to them, not playing attraction game and all.

February 12, 2014

I feel very emotionally fragile. Emily called me to work on a computer problem. I feel that she's taking advantage of me. I would like to tell her that I was happy helping her as a friend of my mother's and that I can't keep doing this. I did say something in that respect but I didn't say it with conviction. I just said I can't keep doing this. I felt guilty rejecting to work with her. I got overwhelmed and it almost threw me off emotionally. I'm not thinking as clearly as I would like.

February 14, 2014

I bought flowers and chocolate for Sherry. I don't want to mislead her heart but she asked for it. She says her heart is already misled. I tried not to talk much about where we stand in this relationship. I don't know what can set off my emotional stability. I don't want to settle for her if I can meet a more attractive girl. My mood is so fragile. It must be because I'm so low on the Zoloft. I suffer so greatly in my mind that it really makes life not worth living.

May 4, 2014

My youngest sister's boyfriend proposed to her last night. It looks like I'll be the last one standing. I don't really care about marriage so I'm not jealous. All I want is lust.

May 7, 2014

I saw Mo today and he fed into my gloomy outlook on life. He spoke about how America is no longer in the lead of medical research. Basically, he was talking about a major decline in America as a country. I asked my mother if she knows of anyone that would assist me with my suicide. I also told my father that I'm ready for assisted suicide. I don't see a life for myself. My anxiety is crippling and I will never get the woman I want.

June 26, 2014

On the train, I was thinking whether what I'm attracted to in a female is just because evolution deems that gene to be fit to be passed on to future generations. This way, in result, it will ensure that my offspring will be more fit to survive. I don't want to be a part of this system. I don't want to pass on my genes to future generations. Obviously females don't see me fit to pass on my genes to their future offspring. Few females find me attractive when it comes to my personality. They want a guy with perceived confidence. The truth is, he's only full of shit. But, that's what evolution wants or deems superior. Evolution wants a world of bullshit and that's what it mostly has.

August 1, 2014

I had a lot of energy today. I rode my bike to Dr. G. My mood is better today. Tonight I joked with my brother-in-law. I wasn't caught up in a state of severe agitation. I am somewhat agitated. I get agitated when I study. I find it very hard to sit in one place and study.

September 19, 2014

I was playing a musical piece of Chopin's and after a while of learning it I found myself deep in depression and very high anxiety. Sherry called me and we hung out a bit. She asked me what it is that makes me not want her but afterward retracted what she said. I decided to tell her once again that I think she's attractive but she's not my type. I told her that sometimes I do find her attractive and sometimes I don't. I feel really bad about telling her that. I don't think I can hang out with her until I go back up on the Zoloft. She causes me to be irritated and sets off my episodes. I think part of it is because she's showing attraction towards me and I am jealous that I can't get that from her. Sometimes I'm able to but lately I haven't found her to be very attractive. Today she was in the three range (from 1-10) in regards to her attractiveness. I should never have gotten involved with her. I just felt like telling her in more detail why she and I can't be together. She kept pressing me for more. Now she got it and I feel really bad. I'm having a bad episode right now. I feel overwhelmed with anxiety and guilt.

September 20, 2014

I'm feeling miserable today. I was feeling so bad about what I said to Sherry yesterday. I texted her tonight and we talked. I started crying. I don't know what has come over me. In my mind I was going to take a break from her. Maybe I am more attracted to her than I am acknowledging to myself. I feel much better after confiding in her.

October 10, 2014

I've been feeling increasingly agitated with Sherry. I wasn't physical with her for over a month during which time I didn't find her to be attractive. I decided to break up with her Sunday night. I told her that unless I can accept her with all her imperfections, I don't think this is going to be a healthy relationship. We decided that I would get back to her the next day to discuss how to proceed with the breakup. The next day I woke up feeling very nauseous and intense mental anguish. I was feeling a loss of not having Sherry. I wasn't able to think clearly about whether or not I should break up with her. I called her that night and told her what I've been going through. She told me she was crying a lot. I told her I couldn't decide at that moment whether to break up with her. We met up on Wednesday and I didn't feel agitation towards her and I had a newly found attraction towards her.

November 10, 2014

Sherry and I broke up last night. I told her that I couldn't be happy being with her without exploring girls I really find attractive. She agreed that we should break up now in order for me to explore those options. I had planned to have a tentative deadline to break up with her after New Year's. I'm feeling very sad now and have feelings of loss. I think that, knowing myself, I will end up alone. I'll live in my parents' house till they die. Then, maybe move into my brother's building. What a lousy life I have. The one girl that comes out of the $4000 dating coach program is not even one that I'm particularly attractive to. Sherry told me that if in the future I decide to contact her and be with her I have to be certain that I want to be with her, indefinitely. I just read my diary to see everything that has gone on between Sherry and I and I definitely see that it's better for me to be alone for the rest of my life than to be with her and not accepting her looks.

November 11, 2014

Humans are pathetic creatures. When Sherry came by today to drop off my stuff she had tears in her eyes and told me that I should use this time to find something good. She's going through so much from the breakup that she needs to believe that good will come of it. But nothing will. I'm not planning on looking for anything or anyone. Maybe I'll work with my therapist a little.

"Our nature takes hold of the choices we make and our consciousness goes along for the ride."

December 19, 2014

Everyone is out for their own good. We're all selfish creatures. We do what's good for us regardless of what it does to others. I think humans are pathetic creatures. We say, "What kind of world am I bringing a child into?" And then we go and have that child. Our nature takes hold of the choices we make and our consciousness goes along for the ride. We are devoid of free will, in most cases. If God would reveal himself to me I'd love to take a swing at him. We, as a species, are fucked anyway in the end. What difference does it make if I die now or wait for the inevitable nuclear warfare?

May 18, 2015

What the fuck is so great about being sensitive? I just watched Montage of Heck (2015). It's a film about Kurt Cobain and his suicide. He felt his emotions very deeply and he wound up dead. He was suffering greatly in his mind and finally had the courage to end his life. I wish I could end my life but I'm too much of a pussy. After seeing the documentary, I feel all the more aggravated and depressed.

I went with my coworker to a procurement event. I was so nervous I couldn't say a word to anyone and needed to get out of the room as soon as possible. I was panicking. I am very upset that I have to go through such torture in social settings.

July 6, 2015

I dreamt that my father was having a discussion with Dr. M. at a town hall meeting and he was discussing me. My father was arguing with him and Dr. M. was raising his voice while making his point across to my father. My father went over to him in front of everyone and kisses him on the mouth. My older brother tried to settle the dispute.

July 7, 2015

I went out on a double date with my life coach. The girl he brought along was Indian. She was cute. I felt like my mood was being compromised during the date. Now that I'm home, I'm feeling really down and set off. I don't want to go on dates ever again. I'll just have to remain frustrated forever.

July 26, 2015

Sherry killed herself. They found her in the hotel room Friday morning hanging by a rope. She was a sweet girl and claimed to care about me. She had said all she wanted out of life was love and she didn't feel it was possible for her to get that. She felt that she could perhaps meet another guy but it would end in a breakup every single time. I was devastated and had a difficult time eating for about four days after her sister called me telling me that Sherry was dead.

July 31, 2015

I often think about how anything I own is mine only temporarily and that once I die, whatever I own will not be with me anymore. I now actually only buy things that I really need. This thought takes away the pleasure of buying new things. I also think about reproduction a lot and how I don't want anything to do with it. These thoughts are like undertones. They are always there in the background especially the one about personal belongings.

August 31, 2015

I keep thinking about the type of man women find most attractive—assholes. The assholes reproduce with women and then we have more assholes. We have assholes in high political positions. This world needs more assholes because that's what women find most attractive. Clearly nature has a fucked up preference for assholes who are greedy and will bring down this world.

September 1, 2015

I dreamt I was with the family and they were laughing. I was very miserable. In the dream, I was doing research online how to kill myself with a knife. I was very certain that I had to end my life. I asked my father for his input on how I could succeed in taking my life and he gave me some advice, backhandedly.

September 3, 2015

I spoke with Dr. M. today. I discussed Sherry's death. He suggested I explore what this means to me on a deeper level. He said he would be willing to have a couple of sessions with me. I'm not convinced that's necessary. But, it would give me some comfort seeing him a couple of more times. It's nice to know he cares about me. He told me that if I would kill myself, he wouldn't feel relieved that I'm not in pain anymore. He enjoys our conversations together.

September 5, 2015

I've been watching my family home videos and finished them. They're interesting and it gives me a greater appreciation for my family. My family is special and sincere; at least most of the family is.

September 6, 2015

My mood started to go downhill after I saw Kevin in his car by my house. He told me about his heart problems. He has a device that's keeping his heart open. This knowledge assured me that life is so fragile and as you get older your body begins to break down. What's so great about that?

September 7, 2015

I read an article on how women find jerks to be attractive. It just reminds me of how much I don't want to be a part of this bullshit world. Let the world be populated with as many assholes from the assholes women dig. A part of me would love to just see this whole thing collapse. I had an argument with my mother about her concern that the light was left on. I had left the light on in the dining room for a few seconds to go into the kitchen.

I confronted her later and told her, "What's the big deal if I leave on the light?" I also told her that what she said came across as an attack.

She replied, "It's not like you haven't attacked me".

"You're rationalizing it?" I said.

I wonder who my mother is. Is there even a positive connection between us? I feel as though she's barely there for us, emotionally. I don't feel I am emotionally there for my family. I am a ghost of a man.

Part Seven

Politics

September 9, 2015

I am relating to my mother more positively. Although, a lot of my interaction with her has been about this nuclear deal with Iran and how it's not going to matter if I have kids fifteen years from now because we'll all be dead. This next war, World War Three, will be the last war because there is no country that has any moral clarity that would intervene. I think about Sherry and that if she had gotten into a relationship with someone, two years down the line there would be challenges. Relationships take hard work. The lust factor would be over after three years and then how will a person stay satisfied?

September 14, 2015

Today would be Sherry's 38th birthday. I dreamt of her last night.

September 17, 2015

No wonder the world is so fucked up—it's a reflection of me. The rage I experience and have experienced is very much similar to the rage each human being experiences. The blind hate is very much prevalent in certain parts of the world. I can't see this world turning out well for anyone. I was thinking about why I get nervous when there is applause after I play piano. It seems it has something to do with myself wanting to be equal to everyone else. I possess an ability that many people don't have when it comes to playing the piano. In a way, I might rather be in an environment that's a leveled playing field, where everyone holds identical abilities. The idea of socialism must be a Jewish idea. My performance anxiety seems to be unusually high these days. When I play the piano, I want to be treated the same as though I wasn't playing at all. It's essentially madness, but all humans seem to be burdened with madness. Humans are a complex fucked up species. It's amazing that some people can be happy.

September 18, 2015

I'm watching a lot of stuff on the news. I really feel that this country is screwed. On the news, a 14-year-old created a clock that looked like a bomb. After being accused, all these apologists, including Obama, treated him special.

September 21, 2015

I had four beers last night and I was crying uncontrollably while watching Cinderella (2015). My crying came out as if I were emotionally vomiting—uncontrollable. It might be that I'm feeling better today because I drank beer last night. When I go through times where I feel too overwhelmed and drink beer, I usually get some relief the next day.

September 23, 2015

I went to Botanical Gardens for an interview to do volunteer work. My anxiety quickly escalated and led me to be overwhelmed. I was in mental agony for the remainder of the day.

October 12, 2015

Mo came into the U.S. from Grenada for his uncle's funeral. He visited me tonight and we spoke about politics. It's amazing how his views have changed over the years. We spoke about the kid, Achmed, who made a clock that looked like a bomb. Mo said that the school overreacted and shouldn't have arrested him. He also said that he's happy that this kid met with Obama. I told him that this kid is Muslim and the school should be more watchful over the people of that faith. He said, "No. All people should be suspected the same." I feel a loss of respect for him. His views of political correctness have made me uncomfortable. It's possible that his point of view has changed since he met decent people of the Muslim faith. He thinks that all of them are not in the wrong and they shouldn't be judged off of the few that act out.

November 9, 2015

I watched a film of the family interviews from 1993. Many members of the family were on my case about bothering my little sister. It makes me think: Is life supposed to be this difficult? It's ridiculous how difficult it is. It's no wonder the world is in such chaos. All I have to do reflect on my life and you can see—I'm mirroring this world. I hope there isn't another one of me produced in this world. I had really bad nightmares last night. It was about my high school principal and there was a performance which I refused to participate in due to my anxiety. I was threatened with punishment.

November 19, 2015

I started taking Rexulti .5 mg. At first I felt stomach cramps. Then, I had a surge in energy and motivation to play the piano. I played well and I noticed an improvement in my memory. I do seem to be easily irritable at night.

"I basically nuked my brain by mixing SSRIs with marijuana."

November 20, 2015

I was feeling quite terrible today while picking up my sister and brother-in-law from their apartment. I had periods of nausea today. It's amazing how this drug turns out to be just like the rest that I've tried. Dr. S. won't see it, but my brain or mind and body are broken. If I had seen Dr. S. before the marijuana use, perhaps he would've found a drug that would be helpful. I basically nuked my brain by mixing SSRIs with marijuana. There is no point in trying different drugs when my body rejects every substance that tries to have an impact on my brain, including psychic healers. It's as though I have developed an allergic reaction to drugs or supplements that act on the brain's response to mood. I don't know how working with a healer fits this theory. Rexulti appears to be radioactive according to the pamphlet it came with.

November 21, 2015

Today I was feeling very bad. I felt so agitated that I didn't even go downstairs to eat dinner with the family. I was feeling nauseous and weak throughout the day. I won't take tomorrow's dose. I'm done with all of this. I give up on pills. Apparently my brain is beyond repair. It's beyond science. I know I'm stuck with taking Zoloft, indefinitely. I am curious to try Cymbalta or Effexor—medications that I've taken with no adverse effect (before I ran into problems with the Remeron and Wellbutrin) to see if it now affects my fever. It didn't cause fever when I've taken them in the past. My body is very resistant to any changes in my brain. I don't think it's because I don't want to get better. I really damaged my brain and whatever is left of it is hanging by a loose thread. Checkmate.

November 24, 2015

My brain is not going to take on new chemical that's introduced to it. There is something definitely broken. I may want to take Rexulti on occasion. It made me feel good on the day of taking it. My brain even rejects hard alcohol and beer. Even though beer is not so great, I can accumulate a level of alcohol in the blood stretched over a period of time. At this point I would get a buzz or high. Of course, I have to take something for the likely headache I'd get from drinking beer. Why did my body not reject the Cymbalta, Effexor and Pristiq? These drugs could never do what Zoloft does in terms of helping me.

December 8, 2015

I wouldn't be surprised if we have a common ancestor with roaches. I don't feel that post-human development is that well-designed, in particular with me. I tried taking Rexulti last week to see how it would affect me and I didn't feel a thing. I may have been more aggravated the next day because of it. But, I had no clarity in thought or burst of motivation and increase in my creativity. I believe I fried the circuits in my brain and if I had worked with Dr. S. before I had gotten into smoking pot, perhaps I would have had a shot with his prescribing medication. Now I have half a brain with no explanation as to how balance can occur, i.e., when I have times of mental stability. I know I'm done. The only thing I can do is to do my time and maybe if things get bad enough, I'll find the courage in me to take my life as Sherry did.

December 30, 2015

I had a very vivid dream last night. I dreamt that I got electrocuted in my room by a hanging light fixture. The pain was so real. I dreamt that I was holding a dog but it turned out I was holding a female robot. She was attractive and somewhat provocative. She was saying simple phrases like, "How are you?" This dream likely occurred because my mother had some girls who were my niece's age over at the house for a rehearsal. When I walked into the house, they all looked at me. Later on, after some girls left, three girls rang the bell and walked into the house. They then approached the table where I was eating and started chatting with me. They were saying such stupid things like, "I'm going to eat that cat", since Ginger, my cat was there. When they had nothing to say, they would add, "I love this house". They were so dumb and young. I thought it was ridiculous that they were flirting with me. Even when I mentioned my age with the hope they would get the point and leave, they remained. They were just acting on their primitive desires; the desire to get attention and to be noticed. But mostly, this is nature's way of assuring the survival of our species. It's fucked up that these girls mature sexually when their brains are so underdeveloped.

I feel as though females are giving me more attention when walking past them on the street. I'm pretty much fed up with the fact that women find me initially attractive but as soon as they get to know me, they lose interest. I'm conflicted about not looking at females as they pass by. I don't want to give them the satisfaction of looking at them, and in a way, I'm not interested in them. Not giving a fuck seems to make females more interested in me. I hate nature for this. All of this playing hard to get only makes them more interested. Our primitive brains react to when there is something that you seemingly can't have and makes you think you want it.

January 3, 2016

I didn't take yesterday's evening dosage of Oxtellar. The damage is worse than previously thought. It seems that any drug that acts on certain receptors in my brain will have adverse effects on my mood and immune system. I felt like I had the flu yesterday. My mood has been disastrous. Oxtellar is similar to the Trileptal which I did fine on eight years ago. I believe that taking Remeron was the trigger for all these current adverse reactions to medications. It appears I'm responding adversely to all drugs that work on the part of the brain linked to dopamine. These receptors have been greatly damaged or altered. This is all due mainly to Jake. While I was taking Trileptal I was seeing Jake. After a couple of years, I was getting insomnia from the Trileptal and eventually had to stop taking it. Because of something that Jake did, I can't use chemicals to alter my brain. I can't use anything for that matter including using Jake himself. While seeing him in the past couple of years, my insomnia and nightmares increased for a period of time after the sessions with him. My fever would kick in, too. I think the best analogy I can think of is that my head wasn't attached to my body before I saw Jake but now after seeing Jake, he put my head on backwards. Everything is out of whack. I'm lucky that at least the vitamin B can positively affect my mood. The question is whether I can accept this new reality that all drugs acting on those receptors of the brain Jake worked on can never be corrected again. I have to take whatever stability I get from Zoloft and vitamin supplements and somehow be okay with that.

January 26, 2016

I've been having nightmares since I increased the dosage of Zoloft to 125 mg. I am thinking more clearly. I'm having sinus problems and I'm trying to deal with them using the steam inhaler and taking singulair.

My father was shoveling the snow on Sunday and that night he was having pain in his heart. He had to call the ambulance and he was carried away on a stretcher. I felt really down. Then my sister-in-law texted me and my brother-in-law saying, "Her father-in-law had to go to the hospital because the boys at the house allowed him to shovel". She was putting blame on me and that further made me feel upset.

February 8, 2016

After watching a movie, I was using the steam inhaler. I started having memories which I wasn't sure was from a dream or real life. I was remembering something about Pandora music station, which I established was from my dream last night. This happens every so often, though not too often, where it feels like I took a hit of pot. I start feeling disoriented. For instance, I wasn't sure whether I sent an e-mail to Dr. M. I have been sending Dr. M e-mails with articles about radical Islam. The latest one was in regards to human logic and whether it's flawed. It was in reference to the discussion of radical Islam where Ben Affleck was defending Islam. Ben Affleck announced in defense of the accuser that claimed Muslims engage in terrorism, "So all Muslims are terrorists?" To clarify, Ben Affleck was saying that it's only a small minority of Muslims who are extremists and that not all Muslims are. It seems like it's an all-or-nothing logic fallacy. If some people act out in a group and we criticize that group, we come to their defense and say, "So, you're saying they're all bad?" I think this concept is way over my head and I can't make sense of it.

I've been letting my hair grow long. I'm not as obsessive about how I look. One of the reasons I would be obsessed with grooming would be to look good for the females. I'm conflicted about looking good or wearing nice things. Until I come to a point of being able to flirt with women, I don't think it matters if I look good because that's not the primary reason females feel attraction to men. The primary force of attraction is character, being flirtatious, being a leader and having access to resources. So, I have given up for now with finding a female. A big part of me doesn't really care if I continue to exist. I have been sick for three weeks now. It started off as sinus pressure and a sore throat. I'm gargling with saltwater and taking singulair to prevent sinusitis. I feel weak every day, usually after I eat in the mornings. Today, though, I didn't feel too bad. I had more energy.

March 21, 2016

I took a half a pill of Evekeo 10mg yesterday. I was feeling my usual weakness and nausea. After I took Evekeo, I didn't feel anything but I noticed hours later that I had more energy, clarity in thought and that my mood was better. This confirms my hypothesis that the fatigue is at least partly mental. I've been feeling sick for the past four months. I thought going up on the Zoloft to 150 mg was enough. Apparently nothing is enough. This issue of being emotionally unwell is now so much more complex than before I tried Remeron and Wellbutrin. I don't want to go another year suffering like this. My days have consisted of waking up, eating and then feeling extremely fatigued and nauseous. Then, I go back to sleep in the afternoon and then at night I fall asleep at 4 A.M. When I went to Montréal in February, I felt better the next day. I had no more sore throat or sinus issues. What the hell is going on here? This life is beyond fucked. I don't know how this world was able to go on this long with all these fucked up people including myself. I don't think it can go on forever. The way things are looking now, I feel we are very close to existing in a more dysfunctional world. I don't value my belongings much because I do feel we're close to something that can possibly take it all away and besides, when I die, my so-called belongings won't be anymore.

March 22, 2016

I took a whole pill of Evekeo at the dose of 10 mg. This time I did not feel good. I felt weak, nausea and nervousness. It almost felt like the Evekeo did nothing. Apparently, I should have waited until I felt sick again before taking Evekeo again. Yesterday, I didn't take it and felt quite good. I just hope this drug won't act like the other drugs I've taken from Dr. S. where I felt good the first time I administered it and then the next day it would turn on me and I would have adverse effects. This problem I have is ridiculous. A part of the problem is mental and the other: My immune system. How can my immune system and mental health be so intertwined to the point where they're both compromised? The Remeron and Wellbutrin really helped complicate things further in how my emotional instability affects me. I also now feel physical symptoms as a byproduct of a chemical imbalance in my brain. It appears initially when I increase the dosage of the Zoloft, it helps with the fatigue and emotional instability but this issue of nausea and fatigue, whatever the cause, finds a way to resurface. It doesn't seem like I will be able to control the symptoms for very long, at least not for the long term. I am thinking more clearly today. When I felt adverse effects from the Evekeo, I had a tablespoon of coffee plus a half a milligram of Klonopin. I felt less fatigued and less nauseous. It does appear, based on all this, that this is a chemical imbalance in my brain.

March 25, 2016

I started taking Evekeo 5 mg. I dreamt that my older brother was holding Ginger, my cat, and was kissing him all over and Ginger was shaking. He was so nervous around my older brother. My older brother said Ginger will have to get used to it till he becomes less anxious. I also dreamt that a girl was bothering my niece and my niece told her, "I have zero tolerance for stress". We, as humans, are all crazy. Ginger is crazy. This craziness takes its form in behavior and expressions that seem erratic and over-the-top, specifically directed toward fellow human beings. It's this erratic behavior that I interpret as craziness. It comes across as silliness at times.

March 28, 2016

Today was a bad day. I had fatigue, nausea with fever and after doing my back exercises, I had extreme agitation. I just lied in bed for three hours. I couldn't speak to anyone. Tonight my mood is lighter. I still have somewhat of a fever. I am very pessimistic about this drug being suitable for me or any drug for that matter.

March 30, 2016

I slept in today because I was very upset after having a talk with my father about my unwillingness to compromise with playing another musical instrument, like the guitar. Also, he was telling me I should do some volunteer work to manage my time. It's too complex for me to get involved with something. My anxiety and laziness combined with a lack of incentive, at least when it comes to work with pay, make it impossible to get much done. I need to be spoon-fed. I did contact two volunteer jobs in IT. I am unwilling to compromise with musical instruments or girls. I'm like Sherry. Only she had the balls to end this bullshit! Today I was feeling less feverish. I didn't have many symptoms but I didn't feel much effect from the Evekeo with regard to feeling wired and my mood was mostly down.

I've been thinking about capitalist and socialist societies. I think the capitalist system is good for people with high motivation. The socialist or 'nanny state' is good for people with less motivation. The problem is when there is a safety net, the incentive to make the best of yourself, to become the best person you can be, is or can be stripped from you. For example, if I wasn't living at home with my parents and was forced out into the world, perhaps that would open up more possibilities. Would I be happier? The kind of system we have now in America has a safety net built in with Medicaid, disability payment and Medicare. Now there's also Obamacare for those that don't qualify for insurance because they have a pre-existing condition. The question is, how far do we want to go? Free college? Single-payer healthcare? When the government controls the amount of money a doctor gets paid, will that affect the quality of care? I suppose nothing will change for the rich. They will still get the highest quality care. The poor or un-employed will at least get some care, although the care will likely be given by incompetent people. The rich will get taxed more. I don't know what's worse. I know I enjoy the safety net of SSD, but maybe we'll go too far with government entitlements and they'd eventually control more of our personal freedom. There won't be any more self-government. The government will tell you what to do in almost every aspect of your life. But apparently people in Denmark are happy. They have socialized healthcare. Though, now they're not so happy with the influx of Syrian migrants. With the socialist utopia, comes the idea of tolerance to all people and then, like all human ideas, it will be taken too far where there must be religious, racial and gender equality. I believe that people should be judged on the basis of their character. When it comes to black people, however, they do commit most of the crime in many areas. Therefore, when you see a black person you start to associate the color, which is something superficial, with violence. This is natural. If you associate a sound with food with a dog, eventually the dog will salivate just by hearing the sound. This is not racist. Blacks have issues in their own communities, like being single moms, to deal with. Muslims, with their oppressive leaders and the Quran with messages of intolerance and hatred, direct constant hate towards

Israel and the West. Change has to start with leaders. But it won't happen because black people blame white people for their circumstances and Muslims blame the West for their current misery. And perhaps they're justified in their blame with the west's meddling in their countries at different points in time. They may be justified with their anger, but as with all behaviors with humans, there are other telling factors, like with Muslims and their continuous incitement of violence and high corruption in government.

In all these wars of ideas, I think we humans pay attention to the research that agrees with the way they feel the world is or the way it should be. With liberals, it's the way it should be and conservatives, it sometimes is the way it is. But these are my feelings, so whatever. The world is just bullshit. Human logic is inherently flawed, so besides for verbal masturbation, it's not useful, except for entertainment purposes. The best way to have a more accurate perception of an idea would be to experience it. The rest is mostly speculative.

April 2, 2016

I've been doing a lot of research on politics after reading up on the left's politically correct doctrine of equality. I've come to the realization that Jews have done quite a number on American campuses with these ideas. The leftists promote these ideas of everyone being equal and have exaggerated counter-racial criticism. And, even when the criticism is warranted, they'll point their all-loving finger at you calling you a racist. Maybe Jews have had good ideas to contribute to mankind, but the bad ones are rapidly coming to help bring the world into ruins. The whole idea of multiculturalism and the refugee crisis is going to lead Europe and eventually America to ruin. The left has some good ideas about equality but, as it is with human nature, they go too far. Sometimes you can't treat everyone equally. The thing is, I share some of the views the left has. I guess, after all, I'm a Jew. Maybe it's in the DNA of the Jew to lean toward socialistic ideologies. I think gays are a natural part of nature and they should have as much of a right to their nature as heterosexuals. Pedophiles, on the other hand, is not consensual and is detrimental to children. Having similar attributes to pedophilia can't be okay even if it's part of a person's nature. The left has this idea of tolerance that is perverted. When a person commits a crime, especially a person of color, the liberals like to say, "Let's look at his environment", to investigate why the crime was committed. The problem with this sort of thinking is that if you want to have a functional society, you will need to control a person's behavior with the existence of consequences. Without them, the person will continue to behave that way. Being humane has its place if it involves appropriate consequences for people's actions. I was out of control with my behavior with my youngest sister and I don't think discipline other than removing me from the environment would have been effective.

All of these ideas are interesting but I think a person's experience makes for better ideas than just reiterating other people's ideas. Jews are so smart. They find flaws in ideologies and gain followers. Maybe Jews really do tear at the very fabric of society. According to an article my father sent me, the leftist Jews are at the forefront of policy in Europe and the United States in terms of open borders. It appears that one of the social programs started by President Roosevelt was influenced by leftist Jews in his circles. Then you have the Zionist Jews that influence American foreign policy in favor of Israel. I don't really know what's true but I could very well imagine that the leftists in America had ideas shoved down their throats from Marxist Jews since Jews lean toward that ideology. A lot of Jews have certain humane morals that are inherent in their upbringing. Currently looking back, I find that my thoughts on the above discussion regarding Jews are overgeneralizations, another human fallacy.

April 3, 2016

I took Evekeo today. I'm not feeling so good. I wasn't feeling weak but I had fever for a few hours. Later on today I was feeling weak and very nervous. I was watching a video that Sam sent me. It was about how a lot of the problems we face as modern humans are the result of not living in a natural environment. Humans have not evolved to live indoors the way we do without much outside exposure. We have high levels of stress for longer period of time than we did 150 years ago as hunter gatherers. People in the West are mostly working too long and sleeping too little. The quality of life for humans with regard to material goods might be good but the quality of emotional and physical health is not. So we are living in an unnatural environment. Maybe we should be thrown back to the Stone Age.

April 4, 2016

I watched a documentary on the indoctrination going on in college campuses. It's amazing how liberals are intolerant of ideas other than their own. College is just a hotbed for intellectual leftism. Eventually, if this doesn't stop, this country will become totalitarian in terms of the people's freedom of having alternative views. The anti-American ideology imposed on college campuses will eventually lead the way to having a president that will encourage this sort of authoritarianism, anti-Americanism and anti-Israel rhetoric. All other views, it seems, are silenced by faculty and students in colleges. It's amazing how an idea of equality can be perverted and be used to promote nonsensical ideas like gender neutrality. Humans are fucked up. Conformity to these ideas will be the real issue going forward. Instead of intellectual diversity being encouraged, it's being stifled and the only speech colleges will promote will be their own one-sided views.

April 5, 2016

I didn't take Evekeo today. I feel better on the days I don't take it. I feel clearheaded and my mood is good. I didn't feel as weak either. I went to an oral surgeon and I decided to go through with having a tooth implant. Initially, I wasn't willing to do anything that involves putting a screw in my bone. But now I don't care. Plus, I'm getting a discount.

April 6, 2016

I'm feeling really frustrated about not having a girl. It's eating at me. I was talking with my mother about my nephew and my mother said he wasn't nervous at all when he spoke his bar mitzvah maamar by heart. I know he'll do well with women when the time comes. I can't get shit. All I have is anxiety. I can't even get over it. Anyway, most females are so full of themselves and are looking for guys that are full of themselves. So, my pool of available women is small to nonexistent.

April 10, 2016

I'm not feeling good at all today. I feel very agitated and hopeless. The Evekeo, like the other drugs I've tried, had an initial spark in the brain and then it appeared to slowly die out. My brain is so fucked. I really don't want to be in this fucking world. Today, my eldest sister gave birth to a baby boy. This life is ridiculous. I don't care if I feed into cultural Marxism, but I will never have kids. Family structure, in my head, is gone. There will be no family, no kids. Let this country be led by the lies of political correctness and continue on the road to socialism.

April 11, 2016

I told my mother, "Wouldn't it be interesting if my eldest sister's baby came into this world as I exit it?" I've been thinking about Sherry a lot lately. I dreamt of her the other night. I walked by her old apartment she lived in when she moved to Brooklyn. I know that with all the drugs I may try in the future, the end result will be the same with there being an initial positive reaction only to lead to a negative response. It's like the lights go on in my brain only to slowly shut off. There's definitely some type of damage in my brain. I'm sure if a test were available, it would be shown that I have one messed up brain.

April 15, 2016

I had to stop taking Evekeo. It turned on me like all the rest of the drugs I've tried. I've been feeling horrible every day now. I have TMJ headaches every day. My mood is bad, especially around my family. I can't accept that my brain is damaged. The trauma my brain took by using pot and repeatedly going into vegetative states, showed itself a few months after with having frequent psychotic episodes.

I really think this country is finished. Maybe it's time for this country to fail, maybe even the human species. I love how dumb people are. It's like the movie *Idiocracy*, where the smart guy from the past would say something and because it was radically different from the future society's speech, the smart guy would be called a fag. Right now, in the West, it's like that. If you say someone from a particular race does something wrong, people cry racism. If you say that Muslims submit to the violent ideology of Islam, you're an Islamophobe. I know that, eventually, a society this stupid has to collapse. And people are bringing more life into this world? Good luck!

April 19, 2016

I took Evekeo today. I felt like I had a sore throat so I decided to take it to see if it would help since now my immune system and emotional health are intertwined. So, what feels like a virus could, in fact, be a chemical imbalance in my brain.

April 21, 2016

My mood has been pretty good since taking Evekeo two days ago. I have a sore throat so I won't start taking Latuda yet. Dr. S. wants me to try it at a low dose but I know what's going to happen ultimately.

During the Cold War, the conservative Americans were considered, by some, to have instilled fear in people with the idea that communism was infiltrating the government at the highest level. Now that the idea of socialism has infiltrated the highest levels of government, these Socialists or Liberals are allowing or encouraging Muslim migration and they will, too, infiltrate the highest levels of government. The Liberals will call this fear mongering, but the first threat has been followed through and the second threat is in its works. I guess the Socialists want to team up with the Muslims because they both want to tear at the very roots of capitalism and destroy the religious institutions. But what will be in its place? Definitely nothing better. Within Socialist governments, the corruption is said to be higher than the U.S. government which has a combination of capitalism and some socialism. The Leftists or Socialists will destroy the family unit and a lot of morals. On the one hand, I'm for getting rid of religion in society because I think all religions are bullshit. On the other hand, certain religious societies seem superior to a secularist society. With too many government safety nets, the government has more power and with more power, they can control more aspects of people's daily lives, what cereal they can eat, and things like that. The Capitalist society seems better for at least some of the population. For them, the hard work, lack of sleep, high stress for prolonged periods of time, all take a toll on their bodies. More than half of the American population is taking antidepressants. Does that mean the capitalist system is unhealthy? Are people happier in a socialist country where they don't work for as many hours a day? In the Socialist countries, however, certain basic items are unavailable.

I fear this country will not do well without religious faith. Conservatism holds certain values that are essential for a moral country. The road ahead looks very dark for this country and the world. The propaganda is hard at work and with political correctness gone awry, people's voices are being shut down. Basic statistical facts can't be stated for the risk of being called racist. Not all cultures are equal, but in the Leftist social utopia, they would like to believe it is. Multiculturalism has failed miserably.

May 7, 2016

I've been taking Latuda for over a week now. I've been having times of nightmares and sleeping difficulties. I wake up at 5 A.M. and then wake up every hour until I finally get up at 11:30 A.M. Today, I took apart my older brothers big TV. I had an adrenaline rush and I kept doing it till I was finished disassembling it and taking the parts downstairs. At night, by the Friday night meal, I was overtly sarcastic with the family. I kept on going on and on with my sarcasm because I had a lot of energy. It's as though the adrenaline rush from taking apart the TV kick-started the Latuda. My mood is good but I feel too much energy and don't know what to do with it.

May 8, 2016

I've been feeling weakness every day now. The weakness seems to be combined with energy. It's like both are going on simultaneously. Although, today, I had coffee in my shake which could be a factor in the increase in energy. I am thinking more clearly. It feels a lot like when I took Evekeo. The main difference is, I don't have fever but my nightmares are more intense. Today, when I was taking a walk, I was getting aggravated easily by things, for instance, if I tripped or some people were in my way. The side effect of feeling agitated is similar to the side effect I got when taking Evekeo. At the same time, my anxiety has lessened and my mood is lighter. When playing the piano, I felt my performance was unremarkable in comparison to when I took Evekeo. I am concerned that this drug is going to go in the way of all the other medications I've tried. I was feeling very nervous last night as though I had caffeine, which I didn't.

May 9, 2016

Today I'm not feeling too great. I was feeling a combination of weakness and energy. I am fixated on a lecture on the pros and cons of being bipedal. The lecture shows how being a two legged creature has a downside in which people can develop back problems from the stress on the discs, especially the load on the lower discs, the L5 and S1. These discs start to bulge and start pressing on the nerve. Eventually, this leads to spinal stenosis, were the discs are squeezing the nerve that goes from your back down to your legs. I feel that we, humans, were never meant to be. Now, I don't feel it's good for my back to walk on two legs. I should walk on all fours. Today I watched a conspiracy on YouTube about this coming election. It was about Trump being part of a setup to usher in a crisis in which he would pretend to be assassinated and Obama or Hillary would become president. It's really upsetting that this world will likely go to shit. I think the Latuda is causing me more emotional instability. I'll see how I feel tomorrow.

May 11, 2016

Today I was doing very poorly. I felt weakness after eating breakfast after which I went out in the sun and felt better. I took a walk to the park and as I was walking, I saw my mother and my sister walking across the street. After that, I started feeling agitated. This trivial thing of just bumping into the family set me off. I felt intense mental anguish consistently as I walked to the park. When I came home, I went to lie down. The irritability didn't lessen much after lying down.

May 12, 2016

I'm not doing well today again. I'm feeling agitated all day. I stayed in my room for most of the day after meeting with my life coach. After resting, I felt a little less agitated. Tonight, I am fixated on how unnatural it seems for humans to walk upright. It makes me sick to look at humans walking upright. They should walk on all fours. Humans were never meant to be. Everything is true and everything is not true at the same time. I really don't want to exist. As with similar reasons for discontinuing previous drugs, I will probably have to go off the Latuda.

May 13, 2016

I took Latuda tonight. I was feeling less irritable today, but I'm in a depressed state. I felt weak today and lied down for an hour and I had more energy later. This is my life. I have this unknown cause for fatigue and extreme fatigue when just walking where I feel very weak and out of breath. I have sciatica now which will end up being spinal stenosis. This is the true nature of reality. It's fine to not talk about the morbidity of life with others. It's like what my father was telling me: I shouldn't put all my pessimism about life and sarcasm about religion on the family at the Friday night meal. I did try tonight to not say any morbid shit. I prefer to always talk about it so long as I'm in pain. Even when I'm not in pain, I like to talk about the morbidity of life with sarcasm. Life is not something to celebrate; it's something to question, specifically, whether something so imperfect such as the human species should procreate. Of course there are those that life works for some of the time.

May 21, 2016

I went on a road trip with my life coach to Philadelphia. The trip was good. I didn't get overwhelmed. Today, however, my mood is pessimistic and I have morbid thoughts. I also feel depressed. My agitation levels, though, are not bad. My energy level is good but I feel lazy, which could possibly be attributed to my depression. Overall, the Latuda doesn't appear to be helping with my anxiety.

May 24, 2016

I feel like I'm speaking more clearly to people and I'm playing the piano well. I don't know why the Latuda is affecting me more positively. Maybe it's because of the road trip I took with my life coach? The Latuda started affecting me more positively since taking it at night instead of in the morning. My mood was taken down a bit after watching the movie *13 Hours*. The American government is made up of pathetic people. The people in the highest levels of government want to be apologetic to Muslims and allowed the attack to happen in Benghazi. And who knows how much truth there is from both sides of the story, the side that claims the attack was provoked by a YouTube video or the side that claims Hillary was guilty? The U.S. government says a YouTube video instigated the attack. Either way, I feel that the US government wanted the movie *13 Hours* to come out because they want to do anything possible to further divide us which can lead to riots. We have the racial divide encouraged by Obama with exaggerations of alleged police racism on blacks. Also, there are lies about Islamic fundamentalism not being tied to the Quran and the prophet Mohammed. The truth, it seems, is not of interest to the public. So why the fuck am I in this world? Talk about the senseless articulation of life.

June 2, 2016

Yesterday, I was feeling sad and hopeless with the thought that there is no future for the world. Today, I'm feeling the same, with it also affecting my ability to play the piano. I had a very bad headache after seeing my life coach. I slept when I got home and dreamt of my life coach. In my dream, my life coach came over to my house. It was the house I grew up in. I asked him if he wanted to come inside while I put movies on his flash drive. When he came inside, he was acting strange in front of a number of guests my parents had over. Then, when he was in my room, he told me I should have never suggested that he come into the house and blamed me for asking him. I told him that as his patient, I don't have to worry about his lack of professionality. When we were outside, he kept reiterating that it was my fault. I told him that I will no longer be his patient.

June 6, 2016

I've been feeling pretty bad the past two days. I watched this video *Why Women Destroy Civilizations* and it took me to a very dark place in my mind. It was especially upsetting when they mentioned how women go for men that display high testosterone. I drank three fourths of a bottle of wine. It didn't give me a headache but the next day, my mood was fucked and I had a headache. Last night, I had a dream about a former classmate committing suicide. He was telling me how jumping in the water would be a good way to go. I told him after looking at the fall, that it might not kill him and would make things worse. He went ahead and jumped and died. I concluded with the other guy that was with me, "See, you can't stop them".

June 7, 2016

I have no meaning to my life. I told my mother yesterday that the water bug that was poisoned on my stairs should have been me. The water bug's purpose for existence is survival and replicating. I'm only doing the surviving part, sort of, but not the replicating. The water bug, in fact, has more purpose to existence than me. All I do is read the news and watch YouTube videos. I sometimes play the piano, but when I do, like today, I am often very nervous. I was thinking about our country, America, and how it is sinking. Before we know it, we're not going to be such an influential country anymore, in terms of foreign policy. This country is turning into a joke and the population is drinking the Kool-Aid. The country will have the debates that the social justice warriors want us to have, but not conversations on more pressing issues like debt and the truth about the threat of Islamic terrorism and the Israeli-Palestinian conflict. Personally, I get confused about the arguments put forth from both sides on Islamic terrorism. A big part of me believes Islam, at its source, is a violent religion and has been for 1,400 years—years of conquest and murder in the name of jihad. Today, it's not very different. The apologists of Islam would like to point out that the West has meddled in Arabic countries affairs and further caused instability in the region. The belief is that the current crisis is at least partly the fault of the west. There may be some truth to that, but Muslims are dysfunctional at its very source, which is their religion and not having separation of church and state. The argument goes, a small number of the 1.6 billion Muslims submit to violent jihad and that it's not representative of their religion and that those extremists hijacked the religion. I don't know that you need to have 5% or 25% to say the violence of Islamic terrorism is due to the violent Scripture in the Quran that calls for jihad. What if it was 50%? Then would it be okay to criticize the religion of Islam for terrorism? Anyway, even though a large number of Muslims don't submit to the violent nature of Islam with carrying out attacks, they still believe in a lot of the fundamental teachings in the Quran, for example, stoning gays, no equal rights for women, etc. So, a majority of Muslims hold radical beliefs and perhaps they are not a direct threat to us. Even so, out of the 1.6 billion Muslims, they say 200 million of those are radical and will kill in the name of Islam. Whether or not Islam, as a religion, takes the blame, radical Muslims still pose a threat to the West. Of course you have to remember that those radicals are following exactly what is taught in the Quran. This argument frustrates and confuses me.

June 9, 2016

Sherry's sister wrote to me that she would like to talk. I am not going to answer her. Thanks a lot Sherry! I'm feeling unclear about politics. I can't think or talk about it. My mind has shut down. I'm going to have to take a break from it, but what will I do with my time? I'm doubting whether immigration is bad and whether liberals are bad for this country. I think maybe we are all wired differently to be attracted to certain ideas. So, Conservative or Liberal views could be full of shit. If our brains are prewired to believe or feel information to be accurate, then nothing is really accurate. I guess we need living proof whether a certain way or idea works or does not work.

June 14, 2016

My mood took a turn for the worse after going to Dr. R. as he discussed my MRI report of my back. He concluded that I don't need surgery at this point in time and that I shouldn't get fat. I have spinal canal stenosis. I was upset for most of the day.

June 23, 2016

I have not been feeling very good the past week. I've had fatigue every day. I feel like I may have something viral but it's hard to tell because if I'm emotionally off, I feel physically off. My mood is not that great. I feel like life is meaningless and that whatever progress the West has made with regard to medical advances is just a fluke of mankind. I am not able to appreciate the things I own. This feeling is ongoing—what's the point of owning things when ultimately I'm going to die and my possessions will be someone else's? I will lose my belongings due to the direction the world is going with regard to the Syrian migrant invasion.

I'm ugly on the inside of my body. My back is deformed with the discs squashed. I've got ridges on my skull. This is what things look like when they're not going right. My thoughts have been more unorganized since yesterday. Today, my thoughts were unorganized. But strangely, when speaking to my youngest sister's friends, I had interesting conversations. It's like opposites are occurring almost simultaneously. The same thing is with my anxiety. I feel anxious around people but when I play the piano, I can play without feeling extreme anxiety. And, depending on the activity or circumstance, I will go from feeling weak to feeling energized. I don't know what this life is all about but it's amazing how things have not gone right with my brain. I don't even want to do the thing that nature instilled in us, humans, which is to pump seed in a woman's vagina so a baby can develop. My line of genetics is a dead-end. This is fine by me. Women don't seem to take interest in my passivity anyway. And even if one did, it could never lead to reproduction. I don't wish to go on with my life. I don't see any point in it. Eventually, I'm going to have to have back surgery for my spinal stenosis.

July 1, 2016

I am done with life! I've been doing worse for the past two weeks. I'm having more days of feeling morbid. I am fixated on how I was never meant to be in existence. If survival of the fittest took hold, I would never have come into existence. It would have been better that way. I drank four beers. I am so sick of this pointless existence. It's a very plausible theory that I am just an accident. I'm such a nervous person. There really ought to be a God. This so-called intelligent design of the human body is not very intelligent. Why is the windpipe and the esophagus so close together where you can breathe in your food and choke on it? Dumb design!

July 4, 2016

I felt better overall, yesterday. The beer drinking Friday night helped snap me out of this episode. Today, I'm back to feeling unstable. I feel like anything can set me off emotionally. I watched this video made in the 80s of a documentary with a former KGB agent. He was discussing the process of brainwashing a nation. It does appear to be happening here in America. I honestly don't know what to think right now.

July 6, 2016

The benefits of the beer drinking were short-lived. I'm feeling miserable and more anxious. I also have the flu or a virus. I've done my best to make this pathetic life workable, but it's not. It never really was. I'm so done. It's over! If only I could find a way to end this bullshit. I'm getting headaches every day from the Latuda. It worked for some time last month, but now it's barely working. I am emotionally unstable. I'm not thinking clearly. Sherry was right in killing herself. There's no sense in continuing to suffer with the hope of having a good few years.

Eventually, when you get older (for women, 40 years old, for men, 45 to 50 years old), you start to look like shit. After which, there's a host of medical problems to deal with as we age. I don't wish to be a part of this existence. The osteomyelitis should have taken me out. I was never meant to be.

July 11, 2016

The Latuda is not working and I'm feeling miserable and want to die. I'm now taking one dose of Latuda at night and then skip a day before I take the next dose. I don't think it's going to work. The Latuda took longer for my brain to reject it but at this point, there's no hope. I wish I was courageous enough to take my life as Sherry did almost a year ago! I'm getting headaches daily. This was such a fucking tease. I was doing well for a few weeks on the Latuda. I've got nothing to fucking say!

July 19, 2016

I decided to go camping last week and on the way up there, my brother-in-law's car caught fire. I lost my tablet, phone and my soundproof headphones, plus my external battery pack and retainers. I wanted to go back to the car to get my stuff, but my brother-in-law said it was too dangerous. This is a reminder just how temporary and easily belongings can be taken away from you. I am not too caught up with feeling a loss because I didn't work for the money that paid for these items and I've been entertaining the idea of suicide, in which case my belongings would be irrelevant.

"I know there's some good in this world but I didn't get much of a taste of it."

July 20, 2016

I had horrible nightmares last night. I dreamt I was looking for my tablet and I would repeatedly find it and then lose it. My mood was very bad in my dream. I was so irritable and had intense mental anguish. How great is it that I woke up with that feeling and it lasted throughout the day? The Latuda will likely go in the way of Evekeo. If this happens, I hope the world blows the fuck up so I don't have to entertain suicidal thoughts. I can't go through with ending this piece of shit that I am. I did not come out right and this existence has been overall torture. I am more than ready to let go of my personal belongings to the greater good of being dead. The world is incredibly fucked up. I know there's some good in this world but I didn't get much of a taste of it. I cannot go through this life without the Latuda because then I would have to suffer daily with sore throats and shit. I will have to discontinue the Latuda if it continues to destabilize my mood.

August 7, 2016

Today, I walked to a café to get something to eat. I had a Guinness beer and was speaking to the bartender. We spoke about Trump after he rushed to change the T.V. channel featuring Trump to the Olympics. I commented, "Of all things, we don't want to see Trump." I agreed with him that Trump is insane. But he thinks that it will be the end of the world if Trump is elected. He also said he knows Hillary is crooked, but she has experience in politics and won't mess up. While I was speaking with him, I was thinking how self-righteous he seemed. I didn't like this guy off the bat and thought he was weird. He's a typical white American liberal. He knows some things, but in the end, it's all faith. People would like to think they are free of organized religion, but they are trapped in having faith in politics, for example, the religion of social justice. People are full of overgeneralizations and I really think the problem with the world is the brains that humans have. It's fucked up.

August 8, 2016

My mood is good today and I was acting sillier with people. I was talking with my father about John's belief in social justice. He told me that John agreed that he wouldn't want refugees to live in his backyard. We as humans are so conflicted. On the one hand, we want to help the poor and refugees, but we don't want them in our backyard. We don't want to be inconvenienced by it. The poor neighborhoods can deal with it, not the rich ones. If the social justice warriors really believe in equality and have empathy for the unfortunate, then these Syrian refugees should be equally distributed to all states in the US, even in rich neighborhoods. If Hillary becomes president and wants to allow 1 million refugees into the US, it should be on the condition that every neighborhood in U.S. cities will have a certain number of migrants living there. There should be a vote by the people whether they are pro or against it. I bet in this scenario, more than half the country would be against it.

August 9, 2016

I took Latuda 10 mg last night. I had horrible nightmares. I dreamt that my older brother and I did something on the Sabbath and my mother was interrogating me. I just blew up in her face and got out of control while arguing with her. My grandma, Helen, was there and I felt ashamed that she had to see me like this. After, there was a police car that was lifted in the air and then dropped to the ground. As soon as that happened, my mother woke up screaming. Unrelated, my mother said that it had to do with what we were talking about earlier. The intensity in my nightmares is definitely the result of taking Latuda. I played the piano today the best that I have since the time I was doing well on Latuda, which had lasted a few weeks.

August 15, 2016

I took Latuda 10 mg last night. I felt weak and nauseous after I ate breakfast. I took a nap and had more energy later. I am thinking clearly today. I was thinking about my possible contradictions with my wanting people to be real with me. I was thinking how I would rather people act nice in everyday interactions than be authentic and rude. I can't stand people being fake, but when it serves me, I would be okay with them being fake. For example, when I call AT&T or any other customer service, they are following a script and have to be polite. By doing this, they are putting my anxiety at ease by creating a peaceful interaction. This goes along with the usual argument of perceived hypocrisy when one person points out to another how full of shit the person is. For example, if you vote Republican but take advantage of welfare and food stamps, you are full of shit for taking something that Democrats made possible for the population. The thing is, why can't one do both? Be against democratic principles of social justice and rake in the benefits the Democrats offer? Anyway, who wouldn't want to take advantage of such a thing?

I was speaking with my mother and father about my niece being disturbed. I told them that she is going to have abandonment issues since her parents drink alcohol. She'll possibly need to become aware of how she feels about her parents' behavior and the conflicts they pose, like love. Does her father love alcohol more than her? When her father gets drunk and my niece has to take care of him, it may cause unacknowledged anger. Hopefully, it won't develop into anything serious like having repressed emotions, which could lead to psychosomatic symptoms. Maybe I'm just exaggerating like many humans do to sensationalize ideas.

August 18, 2016

I'm alternating the dosages of Latuda. One night I am taking 5 mg, then two days after I take 10 mg. I am not feeling happy today. My mood is very pessimistic. I was thinking about how Obama lied about the ransom payments to release American hostages in Iran. How much longer can the bullshit continue? All of these lies will eventually come back to bite, whether in the form of the Syrian refugee crisis or fanning the flames of the Black Lives Matter movement. I certainly don't belong in a world of lies. I'm as real as they get. I do feel I am at the end of my rope with the Latuda. How many more variations can I try with how I administer the medicine? There are still some benefits in terms of my improved ability to articulate in conversation or while I'm writing. I feel like the word 'administer' ordinarily wouldn't have come to my mind so quickly or at all for that matter. But it feels like the Latuda overall is poison based on how I feel.

August 26, 2016

My sleep is messed up as well as my dream content since I decided to start working at an IT company. My older brother hooked me up with the job since he does work for him. The boss said he is willing to work with me with my emotional and physical conditions. My mood is off today. So this is what I'm going to have to put up with, increased nightmare intensity and mood instability in order to do this job. I'll see if it's worth it. My tendinitis may get aggravated from working at the computer all day. My thoughts feel distorted when watching performers tonight on my computer. I'm thinking how the human brain is so messed up with how we think about things and our primitive desires in sexuality.

August 29, 2016

Today was my first day of work. At least the people at work seem nice. I don't sense any ego from my fellow workers. My thoughts are very dark and I am expecting the worst to happen to me and the world.

August 30, 2016

I got really stressed at work today with the thought of answering phone calls at the help desk. I felt pain running down my right leg until the ankle from sitting so long the past two days. My mood is worse and much darker. I was feeling strange walking down the street. I thought about the times in which I lived and how at the age of 35, so much around me has drastically changed. The music on the radio has changed dramatically. I feel so alienated from the rest of the world. This helps fuel the thought of not wanting to be on planet Earth anymore. It calmed me down somewhat, when I spoke to my boss and told him about my pained back and anxiety. In response, he told me that there are the things I can do without having to talk to customers while troubleshooting issues. I'm very nervous and my movements are somewhat uncoordinated. I am overtired and drinking coffee in the morning probably doesn't help the nervousness.

September 2, 2016

I'm not feeling that great today. The feeling of weakness came on strong during the day. I also have occasional headaches. My boss called my brother yesterday and told him that this job is not for me. I'm pretty upset about it because it further confirms that there is no place in the world for me.

September 4, 2016

I have no idea how to proceed with taking Latuda. I don't have much hope for finding the right dosage. The drug always ends up causing problems no matter what. What is this life? I was watching home videos of my family in the 1990s and my mother looked so young. What does she have, maybe 10 more years of life? And my father? Who knows?

September 20, 2016

I dreamt that I was a passenger in the back seat of a car. There was a shoot out on the streets where we were driving. My sister was sitting in front of me. Then I hear what sounded like something penetrating through the headrest of her seat. Afterward, I felt the top of my skull and there was a ridge that wasn't there before. I thought I got shot. My family tried to reassure me that I didn't get shot. In the dream I had thought that maybe the ridges on the top of my skull stopped the bullet from entering further through my skull to my brain.

The End